BAD GIRL

CONFESSIONS
OF A TEENAGE DELINQUENT

ABIGAIL VONA

RuggedLand

RUGGED LAND | 401 WEST STREET · SECOND FLOOR · NEW YORK · NY · 10014 · USA

RuggedLand

Published by Rugged Land, LLC

401 WEST STREET • SECOND FLOOR • NEW YORK • NY • 10014 • USA

RUGGED LAND and colophon are trademarks of Rugged Land, LLC.

PUBLISHER'S CATALOGING-IN-PUBLICATION DATA

(Provided by Quality Books, Inc.)

Vona, Abigail.

Bad Girl : Confessions of a Teenage Delinquent / by Abigail Vona.--1st ed.

p. cm.

ISBN 1590710517

1. Vona, Abigail.

2. Female juvenile delinquents--Connecticut--West Hartford--Biography.

3. Juvenile corrections--Tennessee--Louisville--Case studies.

4. Female juvenile delinquents--Rehabilitation--

Connecticut--West Hartford--Case studies.

I. Title.

HV6046.V66 2004   364.36'092

QBI04-700153

Book Design by
HSU + ASSOCIATES

RUGGED LAND WEBSITE ADDRESS: WWW.RUGGEDLAND.COM

1   3   5   7   9   10   8   6   4   2
First Rugged Land Trade Paperback

To Rochelle, Dannie, Ally, Katherine, and all the other girls who are just trying to find their way.

You helped me and I think of you. I hope you're okay.

Abby

Chapter -12

A THIN LINE BETWEEN FREEDOM AND WILD

Keno picked me up in the right place, at the right time, two doors from my house. I was practically running the second I climbed from the window. I had turned off the lights in my room so that my dad would think I was crying myself to sleep and wouldn't come in my room. He had done enough shouting for one night.

I saw Keno's car. But there was a cop car behind it. This frightened me at first, so I stood there for a few minutes, out of sight, trying to see why Keno had a cop leaning into his window.

Keno was black, and the white cop seemed to be harassing him for that very reason. The cop was asking questions, like where was he going and why was he in this section of town. He then gave him a ticket for not having a clean enough license plate, leaving Keno cursing under his breath. It was not cool. I felt sorry for him and walked out of my hiding place and greeted him in front of the cop. The cop gave me a glare, and I told him, "This is my house, and he is visiting." That was the best I could do. The cop sped off, giving me a look of disgust.

It was an awkward situation. I couldn't relate and say something. I was sure it would just sound stupid. Keno was from Jamaica, in his early twenties and a college student. He had asked for my number a few years ago and we ended up going out for a while. He was a break-dancer when I met him. I remember him doing muscular flips and spins and trying to teach me. Of course, I fell on my ass. To him, I was just a little white girl trying to have some fun. But we had stayed friends. He also knew my age but didn't seem to care. He opened the passenger door for me to get in.

He said something to me, quickly, that I couldn't make out.

"What?" I said, feeling like a dumbass and not trying to make matters worse after the cop incident. He repeated himself more slowly. "Yo Abigail, wha' you wannado?" This time I understood. I didn't know what to do. The whole thing with the kitten left me feeling sick. I said the first thing that came into my mind, "Let's get drunk."

He had brown eyes and big lips. I would have dated him longer, but with his accent I could never tell what the fuck he was talking about. Keno and I rode around in his car, blasting reggae music so loud the car vibrated. I wanted to have this feeling stay with me; I didn't want to go to summer camp. I didn't even want to be a lifeguard. This was really what the summer was for anyway.

We finally decided to go back to his house, which he and his mother shared with three other families. The house was decorated with voodoo-looking pictures of saints and crucifixes. He lived on the bottom level, which made it convenient for him to sneak me past the living room and down the stairs. I understood this since he was a lot older. I didn't mind, I was used to this. I must have snuck Matt into my house about a hundred million times.

The basement was full of workout machines with a bed in the corner. The walls were covered with posters of famous rappers and album covers. "Is this your room?" I asked, hoping it wouldn't offend him.

"Ya. I'll be right back." He went upstairs, leaving me alone in his shabby-looking room. I don't understand why guys like living in basements. They're moldy and dark and most of them are unfinished. I wondered if Keno didn't have the option of living upstairs. Maybe his mother had other kids and there wasn't enough room. I went and sat on his bed just as he came down the stairs with a bottle of alcohol. I couldn't tell what it was and I didn't ask. No matter though, it was enough to get us buzzed.

We had a drinking contest and I won. He knew how competitive I was. I think he purposely made it that way. But I didn't care. It was my last night before camp and I had an excuse to have fun.

After a while we started to kiss and do a little more. At that stage of the game I was a little dickophobic. Besides, he didn't like getting blowjobs or going down on me. I think it was a Jamaican thing. He was on top. I didn't fuck him but it was an amazing experience of dry fucking. The movements were so good and his body perfect. I wasn't very experienced so I don't know if he got off. I got caught in the moment and suddenly freaked out, like I needed to leave. I started to squirm out from under him and he resisted for a moment, then got the message. I knew that I was supposed to be true to Matt but I didn't care, I just didn't want to be there with Keno anymore.

I started to panic. It was after three in the morning, and I was supposed to see Matt that night. I knew I had to leave in a few hours but even though I was exhausted, I still didn't want to go home. Also, I felt obligated to see Matt because he would be mad if I didn't. Keno dropped me off at his house. I told Keno that it was a girlfriend's house because Matt wasn't about to walk out the door with his alarm bracelet on.

From one guy to the next. A part of me felt guilty, but for the most part, it gave me a sick thrill. I knocked on Matt's window and watched him stick his head out. He gestured for me to come to the back door. We met at the entrance.

"Be careful. Don't pull me too close. The wiring is right under the door. If I even go a hair line over, the alarm will go off," he said, giving me a smile and pulling me inside with his free hand.

Matt was blessed with good features and brilliant blue eyes. When I got through the back door, he grabbed me and we started to make out. I was still a little buzzed and I was getting into being kissed and grabbed. He was strong and lifted me onto the counter so that we were eye level. I wrapped my legs around his waist and came in to kiss him.

Then he noticed something that made him pause and stare blankly at me. "What is that," Matt asked, looking at my neck all serious. I turned my head to look at myself in the nearest mirror. I sobered up very fuckin' fast.

Matt, scummy as he was, didn't like giving or receiving hickeys, and this one was reddish and fresh. I tensed up. I was caught. Excuses ran through my head and I didn't know what to say so I giggled nervously. It didn't help that he was standing over me. So I said the first thing that came to my mind.

"Oh, it must be the kitten, I was playing with her in bed and she scratched me earlier." He was deciding what to think. I didn't know what he would do. I mean the boy had an anger management problem that got him arrested and I must have been pushing some buttons that shouldn't be pushed. To my surprise, he hugged me and looked in my eyes.

"I want you to be honest. I want you to tell me everything. I know you couldn't cheat on me, but if you did, I know you wouldn't tell me either."

He was not mad, so all I could do was blame myself. This was an unfamiliar feeling, guilt. I hate guilt because there is no one to blame but yourself. I didn't care about him as much as he wanted me to. I was leaving for camp. Besides, it was his fault; he was the one who got himself in trouble so that the only time I could see him was when I snuck in. We walked into his bedroom and lay down. He held me and we just lay there. He started talking about his parents, and I felt like I had to listen as punishment for being caught with a hickey.

"When I was six, my parents got divorced. Before that, the marriage was shit . . . I like you a lot. I mean, I don't love you because I'm too young, but I care for you a lot."

I felt shitty about what I had done, because I felt warm and safe with him. I didn't know what to say, so I just listened.

"I want to have a future with you. I mean, after this summer, I'll be here for you. I hope you'll wait for me too."

This was too strange to be true. Were these lies coming from him? As much as I would have liked to believe him, I couldn't. And, I mean, as much as I liked him, I wouldn't be waiting for him.

I fell asleep on him and woke up just in time. Since it was daylight, I walked the two miles home.

When I got home, my dad was on the couch sleeping. All my suitcases were packed and next to him. I slammed the door shut so it would wake him. He sat up, "Are you ready?"

"Yeah." But I had no idea.

Chapter -11

TIME OUT

Day 1

My dad and I didn't talk in the car or on the plane.

We arrived at the terminal in Knoxville and found two masculine-looking women right there waiting for me. One of them was over six feet tall and had long, natural blond hair and a very tan complexion. She was plain and looked like a hippie hiker. The other one was short, fat, and her skin reminded me of plastic, which was weird since she had no makeup on. Her voice was like a robot's. She was one of those people who, when you were a child, you secretly thought was a machine. She kept looking at me.

They introduced themselves as Miss Blankered and Miss Curran, "The Village Staff," and then helped me with my bags.

Now sometimes I get a little paranoid, but I think I had a reason to be this time. Something was suspicious. I asked questions about my summer camp, and they gave me the same response, "You'll find out when you get there." They weren't even pretending to be nice and bouncy, the way camp counselors usually are on the first day.

I turned to my dad, who looked as though he was under lots of stress. "Dad, something's wrong with them. I don't want to go there!" I said this loud enough for them to hear me, but they didn't respond. I knew this place was going to suck if they weren't being nice now.

The van ride was about half an hour long. I watched small towns pass by for a while and then it was just a few houses spaced by minutes of forest between them. And then no more houses and just trees.

"Is this a peninsula?" my dad asked, sounding like some kind of fucking tourist. I could tell he already knew the answer. The robot lady nodded, "Peninsula Village is on a point. And we do get to *the point* around here." The way she said it freaked me out.

We turned off of the road and drove up a driveway that led to a small two-story building. The upstairs had barred windows and a separate entrance.

A mixed-race woman greeted us and introduced herself as Miss Fawn. She led us into the bottom level of the building, while the two other women waited at the van. She asked me to sit on a faded gray couch in the entrance lobby, while she took my dad into a separate room. All I could think was that she was telling him how great the camp was, but now I was sure it wasn't. I weighed whether it might be more fun to stay here and shake things up for a bit, or beg my dad to go home with him. Then Miss Fawn popped her head out of the office and waved for me to come in.

"What do you want to say to your father before he leaves?"

"What?" I asked. I was confused. He was going to leave me here now? He hadn't seen my bunk or helped me unpack.

The woman repeated herself in the exact same tone, and I said, "What?" again.

My dad just sat there, like he was caught in some kind of lie.

"You and your father aren't going to see each other for a very long time. Is there anything that you want to say?" The woman said this as if she had said it a thousand times, to a thousand kids. She also said it with negative feeling.

"Dad, what's going on?" I was getting angry.

He gave me a nervous, but unusually firm expression for him. He looked like he was trying not to cry, and that made me scared. He never cried or anything like that. "I'll talk to you later, honey. Just go with Miss Fawn."

Miss Fawn then opened the door for him to leave, and he did. He didn't even look at me. He just walked past.

Miss Blankered walked in the door as if she was ready for a long hiking trip, "All set?" She seemed a little too dykey and upbeat for what had just happened. She didn't even respond to the fact that my dad had just left without so much as touring the camp or meeting my bunkmates.

Miss Curran came in after her. They led me outside where about six other men and women stood. I still hadn't seen any other kids. Things were getting really weird, like I was slipping into a really strange *Twilight Zone* episode. I started to hope that I would wake up, still on the plane and groggy from the Dramamine. Something told me I didn't have a choice but to go with these odd southern camp people.

They led me by the outside stairs up to the second floor. The barred windows didn't make me feel good about this place. Something told me they didn't have a petting zoo up here. Miss Blankered told me to take off my shoes when we got to the door. I asked her why, but she gave no response. *Maybe this is a yoga class. You don't need shoes for yoga.* I didn't like yoga.

One of the women opened the door. There were three locks to open but she did it in about two seconds. I walked in.

Terror, a feeling that I wasn't used to, and that I had never had to that extent, overpowered me. The room was completely white with a desk in one corner. It looked like a hospital. There were two rooms without doors on each side of a large main room. One was a bathroom with showers, and the other was a strange sort of empty, boxy room. The boxy room looked like a kennel for dogs, but it was the main room that really frightened me. There were eight beds facing each other, and on the beds were kids—girls—sitting straight up with blank expressions, not saying a word. All I could focus on was a little girl who looked about eleven. She sat on a bed separated from the rest and she wore some kind of hospital gown and looked like a China doll; she had a ghost-pale face with curly dark hair. Her expression was serious sadness and boredom.

One of the women pointed to a plastic chair in front of a desk and said, "Sit down. We have some questions to ask you. If you have any questions for us that are safety-or medical-related, feel free to raise your hand. If it's not safety or medical, it will have to wait."

Panic went through my body. "This place isn't like camp." I said. "What is this place?"

The woman repeated the question rule, which I had just, obviously, broken. I hadn't heard it. All I could think was how weird this place was, and that I felt trapped and afraid and that there was a girl in a gown sitting still and expressionless on the bed. They *all* were. They just sat there reminding me of a movie that I saw about lobotomies. I had to get out of here. I stood up.

The tall, blond woman gave me an angry look and turned to the plastic-faced woman, "Miss Curran, will you help me escort Abby?" They came towards me so I tried to get away.

The next thing I recall was the sound of a buzzer, like a million car alarms going off, and people running in the door to hold me down. "Get her to Time Out!" someone shouted. When I looked around I was on the floor of the kennel room with about eight men and dyke-ass women restraining all of my limbs. I hadn't even felt them lift me, let alone change rooms with me. I was laid out like a pancake on the clean, cold, white tiles. All I saw were their legs, because someone was even holding down my head with a fat, sweaty palm. My nose ran and I had snot all over my face; I sucked it in but then I couldn't breathe. I couldn't even see their legs anymore because the tears kept coming out and filling up my eyes. This was the worst experience I'd ever had and I struggled against it with everything I could. All that was on my mind was getting them the fuck off me! I screamed for my dad, hoping he was around to hear — he had to come back and get these people off. Then I screamed at them, threatening to sue them. It must be fucking illegal for them to hold down a child. I was outraged. I begged, then I prayed, and I even tried to throw them off, but nothing worked. My face was covered with snot and spit and tears that I couldn't wipe off because they had me pinned down. Fucking assholes! It lasted forever, but I kept fighting. I yelled at them just what I thought, "Death would be better than this shit!" Then I just gave up.

PENINSULA VILLAGE   **Louisville, Tennessee 37777**
PROGRESS NOTES   **HOSPITAL NO. 16135**

TIME: 3:35 pm   **PATIENT NAME: Abigail Vona**

Milieu Treatment note: Problem A (Transition) Patient was admitted to STU at 2:34 pm. Patient seemed very disrespectful, demanding, self-centered, and mouthy. Patient was escorted to Time Out due to these behaviors and refusing directives. Patient became combative towards staff while in Time Out. Restraint initiated 2:37 pm — 3:09 pm. Patient was placed on Suicide Precautions due to voicing thoughts of wanting to kill herself and will be monitored closely to ensure her safety.

- J. Blankered

Chapter -10

FREAK SHOW

After I ran out of strength, they finally got off and took me to the bathroom. It was the only room besides the kennel room that branched off from the main room, and it too had no goddamn doors. They let me take a quick shower, giving me no time to use conditioner. I hated this because the minute I was naked, I was shivering. To make matters weirder and more fucked up, Miss Blankered stayed in the bathroom while I undressed and showered. When I got out I noticed they took all my clothes and gave me the same hospital gown as the zombie-like China-doll girl on the bed. The brush they gave me didn't go through my long hair, which was now a rat's nest from not using conditioner.

Once I was dressed in their blue hospital gown, they sat me down and gave me a stack of papers to fill out about my "history." I was given a crayon and paper and a book to balance on my knees to write on. For a while I tried to talk to the Staff. I cried to provoke pity. They didn't answer me and when my crying became too loud they grabbed me and took me into the kennel room again. They called the kennel room the "Time Out Room." It reminded me of kindergarten when you were bad.

The third time they dragged me to "Time Out," they told me

that I couldn't leave until I made an apology to the Group.

What Group? Those fuckin' freaks? The girls had hardly reacted to all that crazy shit that had just gone on right in front of their eyes. In fact nobody said shit. I wasn't going to apologize, especially to them. *I am in the wrong place — they should be apologizing to me!*

Miss Curran brought me lunch in the kennel room. The food was cold pasta with sausage shit, clearly a nasty southern dish, which they served on paper plates. What if I was a vegetarian?

"I need a fork and a knife, you know?"

"No. You can eat with your fingers."

What the fuck? This place *was* insane. My dad did not know it was like this in here!

The Time Out Room had no windows and pink paint that peeled off around little craters which looked like dents from someone punching or kicking the wall repeatedly. I didn't like being by myself with nothing to do and I didn't want to be in the main room with those weirdos. But after being in the kennel for a while, the hard floor made my butt go numb so I finally agreed to apologize.

Miss Blankered, who had pinned me down, asked me to come out of the kennel room and said, "Call your Group."

How was I supposed to call my "Group"? I guessed that this was them on the beds, but call them what? Freaks? I didn't even know what this meant, let alone how to do it.

"What?" I asked.

She repeated herself.

I stood there for about a minute, looking around the room. All of the girls looked at me, expecting something.

"To call a Group you have to say, 'Group,' then they will stand, and you will express yourself, or in your situation, apologize to them. In this case, since it's not an 'Expression' Group, but an apology, they will give you feedback afterwards." Even her melodic southern accent sounded mean. I was looking at a woman who had held me down on the ground as I screamed, cried, and kicked. Somehow, I felt as if she already knew me a little too well. When she talked, she did it with a familiarity that made me very uncomfortable.

"Group," I said, nervous and unsteady. I hated the way I sounded. They all stood up, not one looking sane in the whole bunch. I didn't know what to say and I wanted to stop their staring. "I'm sorry," I said, ". . . for coming here." I meant it, I was.

This did not go over very well with Miss Blankered. She jumped out of her chair and pointed to the kennel room, breathing heavily.

"Go back until you are really ready to apologize!" Her voice alone nearly sent me running back there.

Back in the kennel, I was getting really bored. Miss Blankered just sat at the small desk in the kennel, and wrote stuff in a pink book. I tapped on the wall incessantly, wanting to piss everyone off. All I could think about was, how could I get out of this place?

When I was eleven, my dad shipped me off to a summer camp in Vermont. Though my mother thought my misbehaviors were misunderstood signs of creativity and something that I would grow out of, my dad saw them as an "obstacle" that I had to overcome. He felt camp was just the place that would help me "focus my energy into positive things."

The rules at this mountain camp were very strict, but there was no supervision, making it really easy to break them. The rules were ridiculous: no candy, no music, no makeup, no watches, no TV, no magazines, no perfume, and smaller rules I can't remember. It cost $5,000, but I didn't see where the money went, because we grew most of our food and lived in fucking tents half the time. When my dad left, they took away my Game Boy, teen magazines, and discman. The counselors even walked away with my mother-fucking lip-gloss. I watched some other kids have the same struggle, parting with their things, giving them to the camp's staff. I remember it took an hour for me to hand over my things, but I told myself, *I'll get them back*. And that's what I did. I got them back!

One night, I left the tent and headed to the building where I saw the counselors put my things. I tried opening the door, but of course it was locked. The room seemed dark, so I knew no one was in there. I looked for an open window. I found one but it was screened in. The fact that they let me keep my pocketknife was strange considering that lip-gloss is yet to be considered a weapon and it was clearly off limits. I used the knife to attack the metal screen, until I was able to rip it off. I climbed through the window, scraping my legs on the cut wire mesh. It was worth it. After falling into the building, I took full advantage of the situation. I made several journeys carrying candy and games from the shack to my tent. And it was free. All for me! I cleared out everything interesting, not only taking back my stuff but the other campers' things too.

I became the equivalent of a notorious drug-dealing gangster, trafficking in things campers wanted but couldn't have. I felt like Robin Hood. I remember some kids saying, "Why are you doing this? This place isn't that bad." But I felt manipulated by the hippies who ran the camp.

I don't remember much from there. A couple times, I let out the farm animals. Once, I opened up the gate, expecting the horses to run out. But they didn't, they just sat there looking at me. Then when I gave up and walked down the trail, they followed me in a straight line. I got scared because they didn't have any leashes and they kept hitting me with their heads, so I ran off the trail into the woods thinking they would trample me. But they just walked to the barn and started drinking from the puddles outside and eating grass. I couldn't believe they didn't go anywhere.

The counselors didn't know what to do with me. That's when

bad is good, a situation like that. Send me home? Make me talk to my parents on the phone? Any punishment was a privilege.

Two counselors personally drove me home before I could do my master plan, which was putting nails in the road to pop car tires and vandalize the signs before parents' weekend. I was the first kid in the thirteen years that the camp was open to get kicked out, and I couldn't have been happier.

And I would figure out how to do that here in Tennessee too.

"Stop tapping!" Miss Blankered said. I guess she noticed that I meant business and that I didn't care much for going out to the main room.

"Why?" I asked and gave a smile.

Then her booming voice startled me, "Miss Curran, will you please help me escort Abby?!"

They power-walked at me, like wild dogs going in for the kill. I froze in fear as they lifted me up and slammed me hard, back against the wall.

"If you move or do any more tapping, we will have to escort you again, and if you move when we escort you, you will then be restrained like you were earlier," Miss Curran said without taking a breath, while holding me in the air. While I didn't weigh much, they did this without trying too hard, like a well-practiced high school bully slamming someone up against the lockers. I tried not to move my feet and acted like I didn't care, but when they brought me back to the ground I was very glad.

It didn't take me long this time around to realize that anything was better than sitting on the hard floor. I asked Ms. Blankered if I could make my apology and she agreed.

There I was again, standing in front of the freak show. "Group, I'm sorry for," I paused. *What was I sorry for?* "Making noises and…"

I knew the woman expected more, but I couldn't think of anything else to say or anything to be sorry for in the first place. I looked at Miss Curran, the robot, for a clue. I guess she noticed that I was staring at her.

"Why are you looking at me? I'm not the person you're apologizing to," she said, making me feel really dumb. I knew that, but what was I supposed to do?

I looked around the room at all those vacant expressions. Five girls looking just like people in old paintings and photographs where they were forced to hold a frustratingly still pose.

Before I could think of anything else to say, Miss Blankered broke my silence, "Group, do you accept the apology?"

I couldn't believe that they were actually about to speak.

"No," said a girl with butchered blond hair.

"No," agreed the China doll, "I think she just wants to get out of Time Out and go and sit on her bed."

I was shocked that they didn't support me. I didn't understand why these girls, who were in the same boat, weren't siding with me. *They should know how much this place sucks, but they're making me look like an asshole, when they're the ones who are fucking nuts.*

I stood there feeling like an idiot. The two counselors looked at each other and then whispered. Then Miss Curran told me to go sit in the kennel. As I was leaving she announced, "Group, because Abby cannot be honest yet, she will try later in Group Therapy."

About twenty minutes later she came into the kennel and told me that I was going to Group Therapy. Sick of arguing, I agreed.

She led me back into the main room where all of the girls sat in a circle with an older man who introduced himself as Dr. Wisely. I noticed now that some of the girls were dressed in dark blue outfits different from mine. A few others had hospital robes like me. Their faces registered nothing and they all looked pale in an unhealthy way. *I was in a crazy ward.*

"Hi, my name is Amy," the butchered blond said. "I'm fifteen and I've been here for four months."

Four months! My heart felt as if it were about to burst. I couldn't imagine surviving here for four months! From what I could tell, all these girls did was sit on their beds. Nothing could make me, or anyone else, deserve this.

"I was sent here." She paused and looked at Dr. Wisely, and then started to play with her fingers. Her skin was gray and sickly. She reminded me of an albino except she didn't have red eyes.

"I abused my sister and brother." She paused again. She had a really faraway presence, someone I wouldn't trust for a minute. Her body language told me she was hiding something, or at least holding something back. She shook her leg rapidly while gnawing on her fingernails. Then she blurted, "I raped my three-year-old baby cousin."

I was right! She *was* a freak! I wondered if her cousin was a boy or a girl and got really grossed out.

"I'm also a self-mutilator." Then she turned to the girl next to her. Now, I wanted her to be done talking so I could hear about the other girls.

The girl next to her, a light-skinned black girl, looked cool and intimidating. She kept looking at everyone, trying to remind them how tough she was. She had big pouty lips and creamy brown oval eyes. She was quite pretty in a way, the sort of tarnished prettiness of someone you look at and think they were once beautiful. She probably needed some conditioner and makeup, like the rest of us.

"My name is Rochelle. I'm sixteen. I'm in gowns for trying to run away but I'm not suicidal. I've been here for two weeks." The way she said that she was not suicidal made me believe her. It was much easier to imagine this ghetto bitch killing someone else *way* before killing herself.

Rochelle then looked at the girl next to her, but Dr. Wisely cleared his throat and said, "Tell us Rochelle, why are you here? Your mom seems to think that you were a prostitute, and you haven't been home for half a year. So why do we have the pleasure of having you with us?"

Rochelle kept her cool expression and rolled her eyes, "Well, my mom is crazy. She doesn't know anything. All I did was run away."

He cleared his throat again, "Next."

The girl next to Rochelle looked like a cross between a man and a woman. She was bulky, chubby and had buckteeth. I think it was the fact that she had more excess muscle than fat that actually made her look so big. She had a thick southern accent and reminded me of a total hick.

"My name is Dannie, I'm fourteen. I've been here," she gave a sigh, and then counted her fingers, "three weeks so far. I was put here because I have violent outbursts toward my family and I hurt them."

I thought how well it fit that she had a boy's name. After Dannie, another girl spoke, but I didn't pay attention, worrying about if they were going to make me talk. I hated to talk in front of people. I started listening again when China-doll girl started to talk. She looked even gloomier than when I first saw her. She was vaguely cute in a depressed puppy kind of way.

"My name is Katherine. I'm thirteen. I'm from California, and I'm here because I like to cut on myself." She said this as if she longed for it, and she had her gown sleeves rolled up to prove that she was far from kidding. Her arms were scarred with old, deep-cut wounds. "I'm also an anorexic and bulimic and have been here for three months." I didn't know a person could be both anorexic and bulimic. You learn something new every day.

After Katherine finished, they all looked at me. Shit.

"Abby, tell us a little about yourself. Why are you here and in gowns this morning?" Dr. Wisely asked as he pulled out a clipboard from his leather briefcase. I didn't know how or what to answer. They kept staring at me.

"My name is Abby. I'm fifteen. I'm here ..." *Why was I here?* "I guess for running away and ... for running away. This is my dad's revenge on me."

I didn't know what else to say, so I just sat there. I didn't know why I was really there. Dr. Wisely didn't seem to like my silence.

"I don't think that just running away got you sent all the way to Tennessee and committed to a level-three lockdown."

I had no idea what the fuck he meant and he could see that.

"Abby, if you rated this facility on a scale of one to five, from bad to really bad, this place gets a three. So you must have been doing something to end up here. What else got you sent here — drugs, sex?" He said this and raised an eyebrow to show that he knew all the possibilities and wasn't going to take any bullshit.

Fuck you. I didn't know what to say. I didn't want to tell him anything either. But something also told me that he wouldn't believe any lies. Anyway, I hadn't done anything that every other kid my age doesn't do. So I thought about what I could say that wouldn't sound too bad so he would get off my back.

"I smoke weed sometimes," I answered, thinking that might be what he was looking for. I didn't think there was any big deal to smoking weed, but I knew it was illegal. It was nothing compared to these freaks, and every kid my age does it. He seemed satisfied with this and shook his head as if to show he was in deep thought.

Then I decided, since I told one thing, I might as well tell all the shit I did, I don't give a fuck. I figured that if I was "honest" they would recognize me for who I was, a normal teenager, not some freak throwing up her dinner, slicing up her arm, and molesting little kids. When they realized, they would have to let me out, so my parents could deal with my minor problems. *They can't keep me here for being a normal teenager.*

"I drank three times, never had sex, but I dated a drug dealer. Also I went on vacation, but my dad seems to think that I ran away."

Dr. Wisely smirked, and Amy, the child molester, interrupted me before I could tell the story, "You went on vacation or ran away? I'm confused." After saying this she went right back to playing with her fingers.

Fuck you, bitch.

"You see, Amy," Dr. Wisely said, "Abby doesn't take responsibility for her actions. For Abby it's never her fault. Right, Abby?"

I looked at him and didn't know what to say. He just stared back until we were glaring at each other. I felt very awkward because I knew everyone was waiting for my answer, and I knew I needed to say something.

"No, sometimes it's my fault," I said in a low voice.

He smirked again, "Well, if it is your fault, why don't you take responsibility?"

He was being a dick. I didn't even understand what he meant by this.

He cleared his throat in a bland voice, "Amy?"

Amy jumped from her chair.

"Abby," she said very slowly as if I was brain-dead, "next, you ask the Group, 'Who calls time?' and pick one of us. 'Who calls time' is like asking 'Who wants to talk today about what they are thinking?' We are only allowed five minutes."

I looked around at all their idiot faces, "Who calls time?"

All but Rochelle put their hands up. I really didn't know any of them, so it was kind of hard to choose. They seemed excited, even desperate to talk, except for China-doll cutter-anorexic-bulimic Katherine, who just looked like Eeyore the Donkey. So I called on her.

TIME: 10:37 pm   **PATIENT NAME: Abigail Vona**

Milieu Treatment note: Patient has seemed self-centered since arrival at STU. While in Time Out patient seemed very demanding. Patient out of Time Out at 5:48 pm. Patient seemed to mumble under her breath. Patient seems narcissistic and self-centered. Patient appears sullen and whiny, self-absorbed and childlike. Patient remains in gowns and on Suicide Precautions due to being considered a threat to herself and others.

- J. Blankered

Chapter -9

HANDCUFFS

Day 2

The next morning, when I woke up, it felt like I had just smoked a joint and the high had hit me, but the opposite. Everything slammed into focus and I realized how bad this was — me, locked inside an asylum with a bunch of dangerous and insane girls.

First, they made us exercise. Like we were in first grade. Jumping jacks, sit-ups, and push-ups for five minutes.

Then they made me sit back on my bed and continue my paperwork. It asked stupid questions like, "If you found money, what would you do?" and "When was your first sexual experience?" I answered, knowing they would try to tell how crazy I was from my answers. I just wrote the same things I had said in Group Therapy, knowing that they couldn't keep me here for too long because of a little pot smoking and drinking three times. I hadn't even had sex.

I really couldn't work with the other girls' beds so close to mine, all of them staring at me. They weren't doing anything, just sitting. No wonder they were all nuts. I felt I was better than them because I had something to do, but I hated paperwork. In fact, I had a fear of paperwork, and did anything to avoid it. I was always excused from anything to do with writing because of my dyslexia, which also meant I didn't have to spell anything right either. It was a handicap I enjoyed having.

Once all of my paperwork was done, the Staff asked me to sit down with the rest of the freaks in the "Day Room." I didn't get why they called it the Day Room. It was maybe the size of a small garage and got almost no daylight. And we didn't sit in there just in the day. They should have called it "The Chair Circle in the Center with Beds on the Edge Room," although I admit that's a little long. This was also where we had Group Therapy. Something told me we weren't going to be leaving this room very often.

God, I wanted to run or do something besides sit. I thought about my dumb-ass parents and how they could have possibly been convinced that I should come here. Like a resort commercial, I bet the people here told them, "The girls will talk openly with the Staff in the Day Room and come home all better." My parents *couldn't* have seen the room that I was living in. My mother would be horrified. She would sue my dad for putting me here. Or she might spring me out like in a jailbreak movie. Even though she was a bitch, she would never make me live in this mental ward.

The girls sat in a circle with their heads down. I felt like a person who had walked into the wrong church during a prayer. I copied just what they did so I wouldn't get in trouble. Miss Blankered and Miss Curran came over. Miss Curran wasn't jumpy like Miss Blankered. When Miss Curran told me what to do, it didn't sound like an insult, like with the other obnoxious Staff.

Amy's hand shot up as soon as the two Staff members sat down.

"Yes," Miss Curran said in her calm voice, not even looking up.

"May we start 'Consequence' Group please?" Amy asked.

As soon as Amy got permission to start, she read my name from a list that she carried around. "We have fourteen Consequences for Abby. First for leaving hair in her brush ..."

For leaving my hair in a brush? What *is* this bullshit?

Amy asked the Group, "Can I have three suggestions for Abby leaving hair in her brush?"

Rochelle raised her hand, "Clean up brushes for three days."

A punishment for not cleaning out my brush? It had to be a fucking joke. I couldn't believe that we were even talking about this. I was getting in trouble for things that had nothing to do with the reason I thought I was here. They hadn't even told me what I wasn't allowed to do. Total bullshit crap.

Katherine, the cutter, gave a smile, which was straight out of a Chucky movie. At least it was nice to see someone getting pleasure out of something. Then she suggested three-minute showers. Bitch! This was the worst punishment I could think of. The only pleasure I had that day was a shower.

We all had to vote, and everyone voted for the three-minute shower. I got to vote too, so naturally I voted to "Remind Group that I cleaned out my brush."

The other girls got about three or four Consequences, but I had at least double. God, I was so angry, because I was trapped. It was like being in quicksand where if you struggle you'll die quicker, but if you stay still, sometimes it spits you out or someone saves you. And my back still hurt from being restrained. I started to cry, and my crying became loud.

Miss Curran told me to go back and sit on my bed. I hated this place, I hated the rules and more than anything, I *hated* the people. Anger surged through my veins whenever I thought about the other girls and how mean they were. We weren't even allowed to talk to each other so I couldn't get them to leave me alone by being nice. I didn't even care that they were watching me sob into my pillow. They didn't even matter to me.

I woke up with Miss Curran tapping my shoulder and telling

me that it was time for dinner. Then she gave me a punishment for sleeping — I had to stare at the clock for five minutes, which is harder than it sounds. I kept on crying and had to stop staring to wipe away the tears. Miss Curran didn't care. She made me do it all over again until I completed the five-minute stare.

I tried to clear out my head and watch the minutes pass. The last time I'd done this was just a week ago. Only it was at four o'clock in the morning.

Handcuffs felt cold against my newly sunburned skin. One was around my hand, the other attached to a bar under the chair I was sitting on. The only plus was that occasionally I ran into a good-looking cop, although I had nothing to offer him. I was obviously underage. I mean, you would have to be a pretty big moron not to know this, since I was being arrested on runaway charges. Nevertheless, it's nice to see a sexy cop.

I was very hungry. Besides the cute cop, the only thing I could concentrate on was the box of Lucky Charms I left on top of the refrigerator back at the cottage where they picked me up. They rushed me. I had no time to pack my clothes and the cops wouldn't even let me bring my kitten back home. "She needs to be fed every four hours with a bottle!" I yelled, but they looked at me as if I was saying outrageous things like, "I need to bring my heroin!" So I had no choice but to give my baby kitten to Kim to take care of.

Getting picked up at the cottage by the police was quite a surprise. I mean, it was shocking that they found me. The cottage was in a little town far from home. The only thing occupying it was us, a big lake, and trees. I knew my mom was to blame.

I tried to retrace my steps and figure out where things might have gone wrong. Last Friday I told my dad I was going to my friend Kim's beach house in the Hamptons, an absolute lie. Kim's parents couldn't afford a house, let alone a beach house. They couldn't even speak English and I knew if my dad contacted them it would only lead to more confusion. I had nailed down all the bases, or so I thought. I even called my dad and put Kim on the phone. She pretended to be her mom, speaking as if she barely knew English.

Everything went fine for two days. We spent our time jet skiing on a secluded lake, doing no suspicious illegal shit that would cause arrest. It was ridiculous that I was being hauled in for this shit and wasting the cops' time. They should have been doing more important things than babysitting me. Despite my precautions, at about three in the morning, cops were knocking on the cottage door, insisting on seeing me. Next thing I knew, here I was. The police passed me from car to car about ten times that night. I complained that the handcuffs were hurting my wrists, but they didn't care. When the sun came up and I was so tired that I had given up on sleep, we arrived at police headquarters in my town. Strange, being relieved to see your town's police station, but after being through maybe six stations I couldn't help being glad this ordeal was done.

I looked for my mom's car. At the time I wasn't speaking to my mom because I stole money from her and I knew that she wanted to get me in trouble for this or anything really. In the parking lot was my dad's plain blue Acura. At his medical corporation he can get any car he wants and he chooses an Acura. The guy beneath him drives a Porsche and he drives an Acura. I still couldn't believe that he could be behind any of this; it must have had something to do with her. He never noticed or cared when my brother or I did anything.

When they took me out of the cop car I saw my dear dad coming through the glass doors. He looked angry, but mostly sad. I remember realizing it was Father's Day. I also remember at the time not caring; I didn't care about many things. This sticks out as one of the things I should have maybe cared about. He looked beyond tired. His face looked droopy and his mouse eyes seemed to pop from his face. The few salt-and-pepper hairs that usually were gently swept across his head in an attempt to cover his bald spot were sticking up in odd, almost comical directions. They weren't even flattened, let alone brushed. I knew perfectly well that he had been up all night with the cops. But I was angry. *He deserves it.* In a way I was glad he was starting to have to sacrifice for me. After two hours of pointless paperwork and another standard runaway lecture, they took off my handcuffs, and I left with my dad. We spent the whole car ride in silence until I reached for a CD and he said, "Don't you dare touch that radio." Then he continued to give me the silent treatment. I tried to sleep but gave up. The silence was too awkward, so I decided to break the ice.

"Dad, I was having a vacation. I mean, I called you. I don't see why you have to overreact. You don't even notice what the hell I do half the time, and when I have a little fun, you flip out."

He gripped the steering wheel so tightly his knuckles turned white and his arms shook. "You're off your rocker," he said through clenched teeth. I couldn't help but laugh, even though he was mad. Off my rocker? It was so old fashioned. Still, I didn't like being referred to as "off my rocker." "I don't get it, Dad. You're the one who gave me permission to go on vacation with Kim's family."

He spoke up to this in a voice with no feeling, just cold: "A vacation with boys? You told me you were going somewhere else, not on a vacation with alcohol and boys. There's no excuse for this behavior. You can't be doing this. You're fifteen. When you're eighteen you can go ahead and fuck up your life however you choose. Anyway, you're going to camp next week on Wednesday. And that's the end of the conversation."

I knew not to talk back because if I did I would have to listen to him lecture me the whole ride home. However, I was confused from what he said because I hadn't planned to go to camp that summer.

I was going to work as a lifeguard. It was an easy job and it paid a decent amount, with tanning benefits.

"I told you a million times, I'm going to be a lifeguard. I have my license and I'm still looking for a job."

"You would probably get drunk on the job, some little kid would die, and I'd be sued for your fuck-up."

My dad had a fear of being sued out of his cardiology practice. All doctors are afraid of being sued but he doesn't believe in suing people. My brother once got a concussion skiing and it was the ski lodge's fault, but my father didn't even sue them. Something about them not properly putting up warning signs along a certain trail with ice patches.

Even though I wanted to be a lifeguard, the idea of camp didn't sound so bad. Then at least I wouldn't have to wake up early and work.

"Five minutes is up." Miss Curran's machine voice took me out of my head. I looked at the clock — time to eat another spaghetti dinner with my hands.

Before bed, a new woman came up to the unit with Dixie cups full of water and pill bottles. Her hair was in a tight bun and her skin had white blotches. She called for Katherine and gave her a bunch of pills, checking her tongue to make sure she swallowed them all. From what I had seen, Katherine needed a whole lot of pills. Then she called Dannie. This went on until every girl on the unit went up. Then I heard my name. I stayed on my bed. I'm not taking any fucking pills, I don't need any medication. I hate pills, they remind me of my sister.

But I did not want to be escorted either, so I walked up to the strange woman. *God only knows, she could fucking be giving me poison.* She put a little yellow pill in the palm of my hand and handed me the cup of water in the other. I pictured the Staff holding me down to the ground trying to pry my mouth open. I was definitely more afraid of having another restraint than of a little pill.

I figured this pill was probably just to put us to sleep so that the crazies wouldn't act up. But that worried me, because I could be in such a deep sleep from the pill that I wouldn't even know if one of them was trying to rape me or kill me.

"Don't worry," the woman said with this throaty chuckle, "it's a vitamin that you need since you won't be getting any sunlight for a while. All the girls take them." I wasn't relieved in the slightest; on the contrary, the part about not getting sunlight scared me more than them drugging me.

I looked forward to sleep, hoping that there would be a way to escape this place at night. And if there wasn't, at least I could avoid this hellhole with a dream. Even the possibility of a nightmare seemed uplifting.

After we were all drugged, Miss Curran and Miss Blankered were replaced by two women with bags under their eyes who didn't say much. We had already been instructed to get into our beds after going two-by-two to pee and brush our teeth with a Staff escort. I felt strange getting undressed in front of Dannie, who partnered with me in the bathroom.

Before we climbed into our beds, we had to take off our bras and put them on our bed tables so Staff could see them. I didn't know the reason behind this, they never explained any of their rules, they just demanded we do them. I couldn't help but wonder if Staff got a kinky kick out of having us flash our bras, or did they think we would use them to strangle ourselves in the night with the straps?

At night we didn't have any more privacy than in the day. Our beds formed an L-shape in the room. My bed was right next to the Staff's desk and alongside Katherine's, so they could keep a close eye on me. It wasn't really the way that you would picture a bed in a nut house — a big white block with a mattress on top. The beds that completed the "L" were headboard to footboard along the back wall. The Staff wanted to see us all in profile.

They kept the bright hospital lighting on while we tried to sleep. When I pulled the covers over my head to block out the fluorescent light, one of the night Staff said, "Take down those covers over your head, or we will have to escort you." Fuck. I was tempted to ask why putting the blanket over my head was such a big deal. Maybe they thought I would suffocate myself or something.

And forget about masturbation. I mean with the bright lights, mean ladies watching you, and lunatic girls dying to tell on you, it was not exactly relaxing, even with yourself.

TIME: 3:37 pm **PATIENT NAME: Abigail Vona**

Group Treatment note: Patient expressed feeling "upset." Patient stated, "I don't really know what got me here. I feel trapped and I hate it. I took care of myself at home. My father was never around. I've used pot and my father thinks I'm a 'ho.'" Patient seemed to take no responsibility for herself.

- Dr. K. Wisely

TIME: 10:54 pm **PATIENT NAME: Abigail Vona**

Milieu Treatment note: Patient seemed to feel sorry for herself. Patient seemed entitled, arrogant, and mildly disrespectful at times; glaring at staff and peers and rolling her eyes when told things she doesn't like. Patient remains in gowns and on Suicide Precautions for being a danger to self and others.

- J. Blankered

Chapter -8

LETHAL WEAPONS

Day 3

The next day I woke up with a bad feeling. It was much more than homesickness. It was probably the same feeling a wild animal gets when it looks out of its cage into a world that it was once a part of.

I wanted to throw myself against the walls until I scared them shitless and they made me leave.

I missed everything at home, including my dad. I wondered when I would see him again. I felt extreme hostility towards him. If I killed him, then this place would probably never let me out, so that thought was out of the question.

In the afternoon, Dr. Wisely collected the Group and started to read from his clipboard. This was interesting because *he* was finally about to say something. Although Dr. Wisely was always very serious, it was almost nice to listen to a voice that wasn't going to say anything scary or goddamn nuts. By listening to him, I felt like I could control how crazy I felt. I just kept telling myself that as long as I understood what he was saying, everything would work out fine.

"Rochelle, you don't seem to own your past. You talk about it like it's your friend's problem, not your own. Are you talking about issues this way so you don't have to feel anything? Stay in the now." He always said that, "Stay in the now," which seemed to mean do this right here and don't think of other things. Rochelle's face transformed from tough to sad. He had obviously hurt her feelings.

"Amy," Dr. Wisely said, "do you act differently here than at home? We told you this before. Make a list of the differences and then share them with the Group."

Dr. Wisely continued to read from a piece of paper for every girl. It was like he was handing out grades. The things that he said were all different, and were supposed to make us think about what he and the Staff all thought we should be worried about. I was the last one left.

I didn't want to hear anything because I knew it was going to piss me off. I hadn't done anything wrong, yet he still wanted to tell me more things to change about myself.

"Abby, during your restraint, that you apparently refuse to discuss, you yelled, 'Death would be better then this.' We take this as a very serious threat here. You are threatening to hurt yourself, so now you're on Suicide Precautions until we tell you otherwise. Perhaps this will make you think twice about violence in the future, towards both yourself and others. "

What? Didn't these fuckers know that the only reason I said this was to get those bitches off me during my restraint?

TIME: 11:06 pm   PATIENT NAME: Abigail Vona

Milieu Treatment note: Patient seemed arrogant and smug. Patient seemed to manipulate and appeared to respond more slowly than necessary. Patient seems child-like, grinning sheepishly and covering her mouth with her hand.

- J. Blankered

Day 5

No one from the outside could begin to understand this place, it was a living coffin where they did not allow us to do anything. Not a single phone call. No contact with anyone outside. Timed bathroom trips. No talking unless it was in Group. Lights on at night. Punishment if we slept in the day. It was like we were captured soldiers in a movie where they were trying to torture us until we either died, escaped, or told them the secrets. I was dying in here.

They called this place the Special Treatment Unit or STU. I hated the name as much as I hated the place. It's funny that for days I didn't know the name. They don't exactly announce it the moment you first walk in the door. For short, they pronounced it "stew," which would have made me laugh, if I could.

They served us our food in bed. Every meal, every day. Ready-made plates of food. They brought it up in insulated bags to keep in the heat, but it didn't work. It looked awful — very southern with lots of fat and gravy, and my food was even worse, tater tots and chicken fingers since I wasn't allowed to use plastic utensils — in my hands, plastic forks and spoons were considered "lethal weapons."

Amy passed out napkins since she was the most trusted in the Group. I didn't want to think about her touching anything of mine, even a napkin. Passing out napkins appeared to be a privilege in this place.

For me, meals were the loneliest time because even though I hated everyone and their fucked up problems, I couldn't remember the last time I ever had to eat alone.

From my bed I could see through the window bars to a parking lot and beyond that, woods that were full and green. Except for a few dirt trails carved into them, they appeared to be untouched.

I imagined huddled groups of kids who had run away from The Village, hiding in the forest like elves. If only I could get out there, I could eat pinecones and survive. Oh, my God, I COULD SMOKE PINECONES AND SURVIVE!

I was never really big on nature, but the color outside was so clear in comparison to the stark white walls of the unit and its bad lighting that I would look straight out at the trees, trying to relieve my eyes from the headache caused by the lights. By looking at the outside, I could make my mind feel different inside.

From eavesdropping on Staff conversations I found out that after you get off STU, you go out to a cabin where you live like hermits did two hundred years ago. I would see them sometimes in the woods. It would either be a group of girls or boys. They always had a Staff person walking behind them, and were in perfect double lines. Sometimes they would carry a rope and a big jug full of water, like the ones you see at football games. When a group of boys walked past a group of girls, I'd get a kick out of their bizarre reactions. They would immediately put their heads down as they went by each other.

I stared at them with pure envy because I missed the outside and wished I could be there. Sometimes I would get the pleasure of seeing a sexy-looking boy. But I knew it would be a while before I would actually get to be with one. I missed having someone to play with, and I even thought about breaking out and finding a boy. I was falling apart though, and I knew it. My eyebrows were getting bushy, and my legs hairy. *No man would find me desirable*. Then I looked at the bars on the windows and thought of the Staff circulating in the place like killer bees in a hive — it would be hard to break out and join the forest elves. I had an itch, and they did everything in their power to make sure I didn't scratch it.

Miss Blankered noticed that I was looking outside and jumped in front of the window, blocking my view.

"What were you looking at? Boys?"

"No," I answered, trying not to look like I was lying.

"Well," she said, stomping her foot. "When you go out to the Cabins, you won't be getting away with looking at other clans."

So even if I got to make it into a "clan," I couldn't check out boys? This was way too much. I couldn't understand how looking at a boy would make any difference. This was some human form of brainwashing. Next, they will order us not to have dirty thoughts! I wondered how they dealt with the boys and all *their* hormones?

"The sooner you start behaving, the sooner you'll be able to go out to the Cabins."

I hadn't even realized that I'd been that bad. Before, I didn't see the point of being good. But now, I decided to try and do everything right once I fully understood how the place worked. I would say whatever they wanted and do whatever they wanted, as long as it would get me the hell out of here. I had thought about doing this earlier, but it was hard because there was no reason. Now I finally had one! I thought that it was kind of funny to be so happy about knowing the hell I was about to go through. The Cabins sounded prehistoric, but I knew that was the only way to the end of this.

This was the first spark of hope I had in a long time.

Just as I started to dig into my fucking finger food, a new girl arrived. The same strange Staff who were there during my restraint walked her in.

She was very pretty, and if there were any available guys on the unit, I'd be angry she came. She had a perfect hourglass figure, luscious blond curly hair, enormous blue eyes, and a smooshed-in face that was tear- stained and reminded me of a Persian cat. She was like a southern belle from a black and white movie. I pictured her walking around a plantation, drinking mint juleps and talking about the weather.

She did everything the Staff said, answering all the questions, softly spoken and polite. I thought this was strange, especially after how I had reacted when I first got here. She was probably warned about where she was going before she arrived. I wanted her to get restrained like they did to me — now that would have improved my day.

I went to bed that night listening to her crying. I thought back to when I first got there and cried, five days and a thousand years ago. I was too tired to cry anymore. Crying just seemed hopeless and made things worse. The pretty girl would soon learn that too.

TIME: 11:21 pm   **PATIENT NAME: Abigail Vona**

Milieu Treatment note: Patient seemed unaware. Patient seemed to break unit rules frequently. Patient does not seem to take the initiative to figure things out on her own. Patient seems to wait for staff to tell her.

- J. Blankered

TIME: 7:00 pm   **PATIENT NAME: Abigail Vona**

Group Treatment note: Patient was not "afraid" to interrupt her peers. Patient expressed "I feel like I can't do anything right here. I feel so stupid! At home I could get away with anything. I feel so lonely. I took advantage of the freedom I had at home. I hurt a lot of people. I took my parents' credit cards, but I did stuff like that for attention." Patient seemed very vague.

- Dr. K. Wisely

Chapter -7

FLIRT

After my jail adventure the week before, I had arrived at home and went straight to my room. The big brick house gave my dad, my brother and me our own space but heat was locked in like a hot box because of the three-layer brick walls. My dad could afford to buy one of the biggest houses in town on his cardiologist's salary but said he couldn't afford to air-condition it; he was a total hypocrite. It felt even worse in the winter, making it altogether unbearable for extreme weather. We lived in isolation from each other until the occasional fight. My brother lived in the basement and I shared the second floor with my dad, but still had some space.

When I opened the door to my room, I was glad to see that everything was in its proper place. I took off my platform sandals, which were not only damaging my calves but giving me blisters too. It was stupid to wear them. I wish that I had spent the last two hours in sweatpants and sneaks, but I hadn't. At the station, my tight low-riders and my belly shirt had gotten more attention than I bargained for. My jeans had been wedged up my ass for a day now, and I couldn't wait to get them off.

Even though I felt grungy and dirty I was too tired to take a shower. I saw that I had seven new messages on my answering machine. Ever since my brother had a party at my house and some of his friends stole my cell phone, getting in touch with me was a bitch for my friends. I relied a lot on my private landline. His friends were thieves or assholes or both and he was okay with it, being the asshole that he is. He didn't even stop inviting them over when it disappeared. Of course, the first three fucking messages were from my mom.

The moment I heard her angry, constricted, snake-voice hissing, "Abby, you're going to have to grow up …" and "You're out of control …" I instantly erased the message, not able to deal with hearing her yelling at me for something that had already landed me in jail for the last five hours. I had been tortured enough, and she didn't even know what the hell had happened yet. She was talking out of her ass.

The next message was from my boyfriend, Matt, who had also been arrested for some bullshit reason over the weekend and had to go to court. I knew that his friends were in the background when he was leaving the message because he sounded like a bigger wigger than he already was. I don't speak perfect English, but talking to him was like talking a different language. I wasn't sheltered, but he was ghetto, or ghetto wannabe.

I was glad that he didn't find out that I lied to him about my weekend. I told him I went on a family vacation, instead of telling him that I was with my other friends. I had decided not to because he doesn't like Nate or Adam and thinks Kim is stuck up. My little getaway was a secret that I wanted to keep. We'd been going through a rocky relationship lately. Between his frustration about my virginity and his anger problems, I didn't want to send him over the edge.

Virginity was a big deal for me, not only because it gave me a lot of leeway to act like a slut but because it made life less complicated. I avoided being branded a "ho" simply by not letting boys stick it in me, unlike the other girls who were fucking and sucking like crazy. Plus, I didn't trust Matt in the slightest. Basically, I didn't want to give him something as important as my virginity. Everything else could be taken. For example, your looks aren't reliable, but virginity is something that's yours to use until it is robbed from you. I liked to dangle it in front of guys who imagined themselves bragging about being my first. I just let them do all the talking and they imagined that I was an angel.

I never went down on a guy but I got eaten out a whole lot. I think that's tied into my mom and how much she hates my dad. I was kind of a man-hater. I was selfish. I heard girls talking about how guys loved them because they gave such great head. I knew that guys didn't give a shit about those girls. That's not how I got my power kick, not from fucking them. I got it from *not* fucking them, from fucking *with* them.

I liked Matt though. Despite his ghetto-fab wannabe-ness, he was really a nice guy. He might have gotten frustrated but he didn't pressure me. Whenever we would hook up he would always ask me if I was comfortable with this or with that, rather than, "Suck my dick." His patience made me want to do more. I wondered if he knew this and that was his plan to get me to fuck him.

Usually I went out with older boys, but Matt was my age. Looking back at him now, it was kind of a cute relationship. I knew he told his friends that we did more than we actually did, but that didn't matter to me. I knew he always gave me respect and just wanted to make his friends jealous. I liked the fact that he was this big mean guy who treated me like a princess. But every day the relationship looked more doomed.

The last three messages on my machine were from my mom, and just like the first, I barely listened to them. Reviewing my messages tired me out and I climbed into my bed, exhausted.

I woke up that evening to a dark room and banging that shook my bedroom door.

"Wake the fuck up, you crazy bitch, your friend is here," my brother, Ted, yelled. I got up from my bed and turned on the light, trying to make sense of what he was saying.

I checked myself in the mirror and noticed how tired I looked and that my eyeliner was smudged on the bottom lid of my eye instead of the top. My hair was in blond snarls from the grungy lake water and I looked like lost trailer trash that used too much cheap hairspray.

"It's your friend Kim and she has that kitten with her."

"Abby, are you sleeping?" Kim asked.

"Don't worry, she needs to wake up anyways," Ted said.

I opened the bedroom door and my brother shoved the tiny white kitten in my face, "Don't let Prince see her or he'll freak out and start barking." Prince was the family dog, a sweet German shepherd that didn't like strangers or other animals and was only allowed in the basement with my brother.

My brother's stocky body filled the entrance to my door. He used his size to intimidate people, especially me. He had curly brown hair and blue bloodshot eyes. He didn't have any style, he had a Goodwill nonstyle — he'd wear anything that fit and sometimes things that didn't. Before, he had used his size productively, playing lacrosse and football. He had had lots of girlfriends, until one girl dumped him for a college boy and he became a stoner. It became his identity after that. He always said he would find the girl of his dreams and fall in love. He had really loved this girl and she totally fucked him over. He started breaking out in pimples and being lethargic. That was pretty much the end of him. By this point, Ted just stayed home a lot and tried to pick up my good-looking friends, including Kim, but he was never successful.

"Me and Kim are going to go smoke down in the basement. Wanna come?" he asked.

I turned to face Kim. She knew my brother was trying to get with her but she didn't like him as anything more than someone to smoke with. She had been feeling even more uncomfortable around him for the last two months. It all started when, after smoking pot with him, she went to the bathroom and somehow accidentally walked in on him jerking off. It was bad. Now people referred to him as "the pudpounder" or "little wanker." Kim wasn't the first to walk in on Ted. Lord knows, I have. One of his habits is that he will be down in the family room at strange hours watching one of his many kinky porno tapes. It's so gross because you can't walk through to the kitchen in the middle of the night without finding him laid out on the sofa under a blanket. As if I didn't know what he was doing when I walked into the den and the VCR clicked off and flipped over to some random station. Right, he's watching a stupid lady sell rhinestone jewelry on QVC.

Kim stood behind my brother so I could see her gesturing for me to come with them so she wouldn't have to be alone. I had to leave the kitten sleeping in my room. I was feeding her as they talked and now she was sleepy.

Ted and I had a relationship like the Cold War. The house was our battlefield and we were constantly stealing each other's things and fighting about it. Our bedroom doors were scarred from five years of this pattern. Dozens of unhinged locks line the door panels, broken from using knives, axes and credit cards to get into each other's rooms and raid belongings. Meanwhile, my dad pretended that this wasn't going on until something broke that he had to replace or we left a mess.

The basement had five rooms, most of which were unfinished. My brother had spread his things in the two rooms that were furnished and insulated. Kim walked in first, and I followed. I noticed six CDs and nine DVDs of mine. And the Gucci lighter I had stolen from some store. I had gotten used to taking a quick inventory on the occasions that he did let me in.

My brother gave the CDs back but only after cursing about what a thief *I* was. "The DVDs are mine," he said. I made a mental note to get these back later. Being younger and weaker makes it harder to protect myself and my belongings. He is two years older, but probably twice my size, so physically it wasn't a fair fight, and he took advantage.

After we each took a hit from the bong, the atmosphere changed. Everything became calm. I watched him look at Kim. She was pretty and I wasn't surprised he liked her. She carried herself like she ruled the world, like she was some long-legged Puerto Rican princess; she provoked admiration wherever she went.

Weed was the only positive thing in my brother's and my relationship. We would smoke whenever his friends weren't around, which was usually when he just woke up. Days after he started smoking, I smoked with him for my first time. I don't know why my brother smoked me up the first time. Ever since then, it had been our bonding activity. This sibling bonding excluded my sister — she didn't live with us and she would overdose if she took any more goddamn drugs anyway. She had to be constantly taking prescription pills to stop the voices in her head. If she didn't she would have paranoid outbursts and throw crazy fits.

I felt better now. I wanted to spend the week either clubbing or getting high, which were the things I did best.

TIME: 3:21 pm   **PATIENT NAME: Abigail Vona**

Individual Psychotherapy note: Patient expressed "My father lied to me. I feel abandoned. I never told my father where I was going.

I didn't think he cared. I got into a lot of fights with my parents. I walked out of school to go shop. I don't want to kill myself. I'm scared of dying and things like needles and stuff. People treat me like I'm suicidal. They are mean to me here. My father thinks I do a lot more than I really do because I date older guys. I'm depressed, stupid and superficial. I don't even know who I am. I over-react to a lot of things. My father ditched me here. My parents have always ditched me. My mother and father talk about each other to me. They are awful with that. They put each other down. All my friends are superficial. Sometimes I think I'm the prettiest girl in the world, and others I think I'm the ugliest. My moods are awful." Patient seemed tearful and picked at her nails.

- Dr. K. Wisely

Day 7

"You can put your heads up now and begin Group. Who wants to 'Check In' first?"

Amy started off as though it was a race with words in which she alone was competing. "I thought a lot about the Focus I got and what it said." She looked down at the ground. She shifted in her chair and fidgeted with her thumbs. "I really don't know why I act so well here. I guess, in a way, it's because I get treated so well." She looked at Dr. Wisely, then at the Group, to see if we were satisfied with what she said. "Anyone else want to talk?"

Dr. Wisely grunted, "Amy, tell us what really happened with your cousin."

Amy's hand nervously went up to her mouth. She started to gnaw on it, looking petrified. She was creepy-looking with her bony fingers and her pasty gray skin.

"I . . . I . . . I don't really know why I did it. And like I said before, I played with his privates, I know I shouldn't have done it and then he went and told his mother."

"You did this in front of your sister?" Dr. Wisely asked.

Amy's dumbfounded look turned fearful. "Yeah?" she said, probably realizing that Dr. Wisely had been tipped off about the sister by her family.

"Why?" he asked.

"I don't know, I just did I guess."

"Maybe to upset your sister? To make her feel like she had no control? Make her realize you controlled everything? Or maybe you were just jealous?"

Amy sat there with her head down like she was in a trance. A minute passed before she asked, "Who else calls time?"

Suddenly Amy seemed happy again, having the power to pick, and of course she took a long time. She got real pleasure from it. I hadn't noticed before that Amy *was* a control freak like Dr. Wisely had said!

Katherine told how she loved to throw up food, saying how much control she felt and how all her bad feelings would disappear whenever she did it. She would even throw up her own spit after she chewed gum. And cutting did the same thing for her. She told how when she went out, she would put glass in her water, so she could cut on herself in her mouth and no one would know. Her mom would always find knives in the house and wonder why they were lying around. Katherine then called on me for "Check In." We all had to do it.

I stared at my feet, trying to buy some time, thinking about what to say. I decided to just shut my mouth. *This will show the Staff that I don't have any problems and then I can go home. If I tell them how fucking scared I am, then I'm not being perfect, I'm not being good, plus I don't have anything really wrong with me, like cutting or anything. The suicide thing makes me so angry. If I speak I don't know what I will get in trouble for next.*

"I'm feeling fine," I said quickly, "and I don't want to speak." The whole Group looked at me as though *I* was the crazy one.

Dr. Wisely raised his eyebrows at me. "Rochelle?" he said.

Rochelle took a deep breath, like she was going under water and needed to preserve her oxygen. She looked at her feet and said, "I had sex for money, okay?" She said this so fast we barely heard it. She looked around.

"Would anyone else like to talk?" she asked hesitantly.

Dr. Wisely seemed pleased that Rochelle came clean, but not pleased that she didn't want to talk about it more. I wouldn't want to tell anyone about that stuff if I were her. I looked around the circle and thought: they should have the right to do drugs, be prostitutes, and cut on themselves if that's what they wanted to do. It wasn't anyone's business, and we live in a fucking free country. I was even about to say this out loud, but suddenly I thought of them putting me in the kennel, or even worse — restraints.

I thought about Rochelle and I wondered how many secrets she had. I was curious to know just how bad of a prostitute she was. Was it one-night-stand stuff or did she have a pimp along with hourly rates?

Seeing Dr. Wisely's disappointment, Rochelle took another breath. Good, I really wanted to hear this.

"Okay, I'm going to tell how I got into prostitution. See, I didn't just wake up one day and say, hey, I'm going to the streets to sell my body now. What it came down to was, I wanted to earn extra money, and so my friend hooked me up with work. I was too young to get most jobs, but with a little makeup and a fake ID, I could be a stripper. So that's exactly what I did."

Rochelle talked about how she scored the job, loved the

lifestyle, liked the men wanting her, and then how one day she met this guy named Joaquin who came up with a brilliant plan to open up a business. She would be the partner *and* the merchandise.

Rochelle talked about this with no regret or self-pity, as if she was telling the story about a friend. She had started to change a lot on the unit too. She wasn't acting like she just came from the 'hood, but seemed more fragile and childlike. It was strange, but I liked her.

I was still thinking about Rochelle when the new girl started talking. At first, she stuck out like an angel who had just strolled through the gates of hell. But she reminded me of that guy who massacred forty-five people — everyone, even his neighbors, thought he was the nicest man around. Mary seemed exactly like that kind of person — sweet, but the opposite once you got to know her. She smiled at the Staff, as if to flirt with them and always said, "Yes, ma'am," "No, ma'am," while batting her eyelashes.

I wondered if she thought all the Staff were lesbians, and that if she flirted with them, they would let her go. I didn't blame her. If someone said, "Do this, and I'll let you out," I know I would have done it, no matter how unpleasant it was. *Anything to get out of this place.* I would rather do it with male Staff but it didn't matter, I would have eaten all the Staff's pussy to get out.

"Hi! My name is Mary." God, she acted like such a fucking priss. Sweet Mary with her thick accent and darling eyes.

"I've been here, well . . . I guess I've been here thirteen hours." She laughed as though this was funny, but it wasn't a mocking laugh or an evil laugh, just a sweet-faced laugh that nobody understood. I don't think any of us had seen anything like it.

"I'm seventeen, and I'm here for taking the car without permission when there was an emergency!"

Dr. Wisely laughed sarcastically, but Mary didn't catch on to the sarcasm and saw this as the perfect opportunity to suck up.

"We're just going to have to call you Saint Mary, the first saint to ever hit STU!" said Dr. Wisely, who did not mean it at all.

But she went on laughing with him. When Dr. Wisely noticed Mary go to a new level of ass-kissing, he stopped laughing abruptly. "Mary, we all know that you're not so nice, so stop flirting with me. And I wasn't laughing with you — I was laughing at you, so cut the bullshit."

Horror fell over Mary's face, and it reminded me of the exact moment I had walked into this hellhole. I guess it just took her longer to realize that she was trapped. She began to cry, but her tears didn't strike me as genuine. Mary was obviously trying to make us feel bad for her but it was far too late for any of that shit. You don't get any points here for dishonesty. Her tears were as fake as her laugh and her smile. Fuck her.

After Group, Dr. Wisely took his clipboard and two chairs into the kennel room. He saw people privately there, like it was his office. After seeing Amy and Rochelle, he called for me.

I walked into the narrow room. At least I didn't have to sit on the cold floor this time.

"So, Abby, how are you feeling?"

"I feel off the charts bad, horrible. This suicide thing is really bothering me, 'cause I'm not."

"Well, you made a death threat."

He had a point, but he wasn't thinking about the fact that I had ten people holding me down.

"I suggest you don't make any more of them. Now, your parents told me that you complained about being depressed."

This was true, but I didn't know what depression was until I came here. Besides, I told my parents that because I wanted to get prescription pills so I could sell them. But I didn't really pursue this with Dr. Wisely.

He gave me a short list of meds I could try to help my "depression." I only recognized the name Paxil because I had seen it on television commercials — it was some woman looking out a window but scared to go outside, and then she's outside playing with her kids. It was like, "Paxil, a miracle pill that takes care of a lot of stuff." I left the meeting agreeing to take Paxil.

When the pill lady arrived that night, I wished that my green pill would kick in and knock me out, or at least let me look at this unit positively, but no pill could do that. I wondered what made the Paxil woman so goddamn happy in the commercial.

TIME: 2:58 pm   **PATIENT NAME: Abigail Vona**

Group Treatment note: Patient was playing with her hair while a peer was speaking and was directed by staff to at least act as though she was paying attention. Patient complied but tried to justify her actions. Patient did not discuss her issues at this time.

                              - Dr. K. Wisely

Chapter -6

PUSSY

The day before I left for Tennessee I was woken up by the kitten pawing my face and meowing. The kitten was the closest thing I had to an alarm clock and she needed to be fed a half dozen times a day. It was a bit annoying to be woken up so early, but she was an adorable baby so it didn't bother me too much. Some little kids had found her on the side of the road and asked me to take her, saying that they couldn't take care of a kitten because their parents hated cats. She was so little and cute that I couldn't say no. She had been living with me for two weeks now and I enjoyed watching her get stronger every day. I had decided to give her to my aunt, who loves animals, when I went to summer camp.

Later that day I got a call from Matt, who told me the rest of the story about his run-in with the law. He was now on house arrest for punching some kids. It was one of those petty fights that he would get into that would usually turn physical. He explained how he couldn't leave the house and that he had a mechanical bracelet which let the cops know his every move. He insisted that I come over that night. He knew my history of going away to summer camp so he was shocked that my parents would bother to try sending me again. At the same time, he knew how crazy they were.

Later that evening, as I was packing a toothbrush and my makeup to go to Matt's house, Nate called. He told me about a hot club that he could get me into because his brother knew one of the bouncers. Ever since I lost my fake ID I was reluctant to go to clubs because getting in became a hassle. I didn't think twice about saying yes and changing my plans to go to the club and party with all of my friends for the last night in Connecticut before camp, rather than go to my boyfriend's house to become his love slave.

Around midnight, I left the kitten in my room and went to meet Nate, Adam, and Anastasia at the local park. I told them not to come to my house, just in case my dad decided to play drill sergeant and hassle me. Adam and Nate were in the front seat rolling a blunt, and Anastasia sat in the back seat shaking her head in disapproval. Nate's slender fingers quickly softened the paper around the weed. His dirty blond hair was almost shoulder length and pushed behind his ears. He squinted his yellow-green eyes, concentrating on what he was doing. If I didn't know his reputation I would think he was cute. I was glad Adam wasn't the one rolling the blunt. He usually slobbers all over the paper and when you put your lips on it you taste a mixture of cigarette paper and spit.

Anastasia was by far the prettiest girl in my high school, but she didn't seem aware of her great looks and how much guys adored her. Her eyes were cat-like, her lips full, her cheek bones were set high, her nose perfect, and her wavy brown hair flowed like silk. She didn't smoke and rarely drank, so I wondered why she was going to the club since she wasn't a partier.

"I heard about your dad flipping out," she said as I got into the car.

"I told Anastasia about the cops scaring the shit out of us at the cottage," Adam said as he started to light the blunt. "I thought they came to the house because of the neighbors complaining. And

I'm still thanking God that they didn't see the ounce of weed on the kitchen table."

"That whole camp thing in Knoxville, that's a drag," Anastasia said. She gave Adam a disgusted look when he offered her a hit. I took the joint instead.

When we arrived in front of the club, Nate handed me a yellow pill. "Take this, it's like a whole other world." He sounded like the smarmy drug dealer on an after-school special. A whole new world? Investigating a new world is a nice way of deciding to go crazy. To take a pill to make you crazy, even temporarily out of your mind, didn't sound like fun. "No," I said, trying to suppress my anger, "I don't like hallucinogens." What I really meant was that I didn't like the *idea* of hallucinogens. I lived half my life with my older sister who was insane. I didn't need to add myself to that list.

"Chill," Nate said. "It's not acid and all it does is make you chill out a bit."

"What is it then?"

"Ecstasy, that's all."

Adam and Nate were known for taking not only "E" but acid and a variety of other prescription medication, so I had to ask. "Whenever a desperate guy wants an excuse to get physical, they offer 'E' which makes you horny," I said, watching him turn to Anastasia.

She shook her head, laughing before he could even ask. "You know with 'E' your dick won't work. You think girls want you if your dick won't work? I don't think so, honey."

After Anastasia said this, they didn't tell us when they were taking it, as if it would have mattered. We weren't ever going to be interested in either of them.

Nate thought of himself as the pimp of our town. He had dropped out of high school and worked for his father, driving around in his ride doing drugs all day. He had been with all of my friends and cheated on all of them; he looked at love like a poker game.

Like Nate said, he knew the bouncer, and in no time we were in the club. The club was pretty big, it was a one-room building that looked like it used to be a warehouse until they stuck a disco ball on the ceiling and put a bar in. It wasn't exactly Studio 54, but people were already crowding in. Anastasia and I started to dance in the middle of the floor while Adam and Nate went to the bar to wash down their pills. I wasn't much of a drinker and Anastasia decided not to drink after seeing Nate's suspicious behavior. "He might rape us later tonight if we don't stick together," she laughed.

"Or he might at least try!" I laughed too.

After dancing a while, we wanted to go. The club was filling up with drunk men twice our age and bimbo stripper-types were pushing us off the floor. One especially creepy man with a huge beer belly slapped Anastasia on the ass, causing her to yelp. He came over to me, touched my hair and said, "You two are the hottest little pussycats in the club." Despite the attention we were getting, this was not really our style.

Anastasia and I walked as fast as we could through the crowded dance floor. We ran into Adam, who was dancing with a girl with fake blond hair and dark black roots. Her ass was in the air as she rubbed up and down on Adam's crotch. I tapped him on the back and when she saw me she started rubbing against another guy.

"What do you want?" Adam said with an expression of, *You're ruining my game!*

Once he realized that she wasn't coming back, the three of us then went looking for Nate, our source of transportation. We couldn't find him for a long time. Just as we started to panic, since all three of us were fifteen and none of us had a car, he came up from behind. "Boo," he said, giving me a hug.

"We want to leave this place, it's fucking weird," I said, noticing how out of it he seemed.

Nate drove us home, but he was so drunk, I actually worried – I did not want to see more cops this week. They dropped me off at my house first. Nate had to park the car in front of my neighbor's house, just in case my dad was up. As I walked up to the house, I noticed that the lights in my dad's room were still on and so were mine, even though I had turned them off. I opened the window and climbed in, making sure not to wake anyone. I had to pry open the window with a garden shovel in order to fit myself in. I hadn't had the keys for a while. I was proud of how good I was at breaking and entering, even if it was my own house.

When I got into my room, the lights were on and the message light was flashing. I punched the button and leaned on the desk to listen. I had turned the sound way down so I wouldn't wake anyone up. It was Keno, my old flame. "'Dis is Keno. Just callin' t'see what you up to later. Get back to me." I had trouble understanding the message because of his thick Jamaican accent, but I got the idea. Despite our communication problems, we never had any trouble making plans. As the message ended, the door swung open.

"You!" My dad glared at me as if saying, *You know what you did!* I noticed he was teary-eyed. "You took a life, you're really sick."

I just stood there wondering what the fuck he was talking about and if he was going through some kind of breakdown. "The kitten is dead! You killed the kitten! Abby, I don't even know what to think of you anymore ... I don't know who you are."

I couldn't believe it. I had no idea what he was talking about. I hadn't killed anything. "Get the fuck out of my room!" I tried to shout but couldn't find my voice. I pushed him towards the door and closed it behind him. I could hear him yelling in the hall, "You should have been here taking care of your kitten!"

I looked at the blanket on my bed and didn't see anything. No kitten. *It can't be dead.* So where the fuck was it? Why did he say that? I needed to find my kitten. I wished I had stayed and hadn't gone to the club. I heard footsteps behind me but didn't want to look up, instead I searched for the kitten.

"He told you, it's dead." I turned around and my brother was standing over me. His face showed a disgust that made his jaw hang and his teeth show. His hands were in his pockets, making his shoulders hunch as he leaned over me. I felt small, sick, and dizzy now too. "Dad and I found Prince up here playing with its mangled body. You left your door open."

I couldn't believe it. I kept looking, hoping to wake up from this nightmare. It just shouldn't be this way. *It just hasn't happened*, I kept telling myself.

"Dad insisted on cleaning up the mess. The blood was all over the hallway. You're a fuckin' animal killer," he said and walked out of the room, turning off the light. I wanted to yell at him to turn it back on again but I didn't have the energy. I felt numb except for my stomach, which seemed to be tearing in half. I couldn't bring myself to look, but I also didn't believe it. I was actually grateful for the dark as I sat there wondering what to do next. I couldn't stand the idea of seeing Matt because I didn't want to talk or be hassled, but I had to get out of here.

I called Keno. He would come over and pick me up.

TIME: 2:55 pm   **PATIENT NAME: Abigail Vona**

Milieu Treatment note: Patient does not follow directives and rules well. Statements are repeated to her several times. Patient seems to act dumb. Patient states "I'm stupid. I don't spend much time thinking. I'm not smart, I don't like having burdens on me." Patient seems very superficial. Patient remains in gowns and on Suicide Preventions due to being a danger to herself.

- R. Curran

TIME: 4:17 pm   **PATIENT NAME: Abigail Vona**

Group Treatment note: Patient expressed feeling "hopeful, proud." Patient discussed feelings for her father stating, "When my father lies about not having money, it makes me want to steal from him. It makes me angry. I feel like I never have to grow up and can always live off his money." Patient seems to want to talk instead of listen.

- Dr. K. Wisely

Day 14

"Come up, Abby. It's time for your Family Therapy," said Miss Blankered monotonously.

I jumped off my bed with a huge smile. This was the most exciting thing to happen since I had arrived. The closest thing I had felt to excitement so far was getting extra Equal for my cereal.

Maybe my dad will take me out of here. But I knew that was wishful thinking. Then I thought about acting bad. *He might see that this isn't working and take me out. Or maybe I should act good, and he will take me out because I'm fixed.* I contemplated what I should do and knew this was important. Then it came to me. *I will make him feel sorry for me.*

Two weeks ago, I would think of a meeting with my dad as something to dread. Now, it was the best thing to happen in my life. *God, how pathetic I've become.*

Miss Blankered and Miss Curran grabbed each of my arms and walked me out the door, like gentlemen do with maidens in old movies, only I was in a hospital gown, and they were far from gentlemen. I wondered if they enjoyed restraining kids, or took some sadistic pleasure from it, or whether they went home and told themselves how much they were helping out messed-up kids. They took me to the downstairs part of the building. I thought this was funny considering I had just spent two solid weeks upstairs, and had never seen downstairs except for when I first arrived.

In an office, a woman was talking on the phone. It was the same mixed-race woman who was there when I first came in. She was dressed like a flower child. Her shirt-sleeves looked like folded bells, and her flower-patterned skirt touched the ground. A true hippie chick.

She gazed at me, and said into the phone, "Well, Abby is here."

She pointed to a chair, motioning for me to sit down. Before I could, Miss Blankered and Miss Curran came along and shoved me into it. They then walked out, leaving me there alone with this strange woman on the phone.

Now's the time, I can run. But I thought twice about it. *They might be thinking I will do it. This could be a trap.*

The woman stopped talking on the phone and looked straight at me. "Hi, my name's Miss Fawn, and I'll be your Family Therapist for your stay at The Village."

She said this in a pleasant voice, unlike the Staff that talked down to me.

"You can pick up the phone if you like," she said. "Your dad's on it."

I stared at her. A phone call? I thought he was going to be here! This completely crushed me and ruined my plans.

The phone felt heavy in my hands and looked alien. It seemed like forever since I had last used one. I held it to my ear and just sat there. I had no idea what to say.

"Hi, Abby. You there?" My dad asked as though nothing had happened, like he was the same old dad, as if I wasn't in some mental asylum, as if he wasn't the worst dad on planet fucking Earth.

I wanted to kill him, but he was home, miles away. And I was stuck in some weird-ass hospital robe. I couldn't even talk to people, except about my problems. *But I don't have any problems. I am different from these freaks.* I wanted to say all this and more, but all I could do was just sit there.

"Yeah," I said with no expression, "I'm here." I started to cry. There was an awkward pause as none of us knew what to say. Holding back anger wasn't something I was used to. I wanted to tell him how unfair all this was. How it was all a mistake and how Ted should have been here instead. *He* was the one who smoked me up the first time. *He* was the one who bullied me and took advantage of me, but my dad would always say, "When a fight breaks out you're both to blame," then he'd go ahead and punish *me*. It was the easy thing for him to do because he never stood up to my brother, because of his size and because Ted is the son.

I thought about not speaking to my dad, and becoming like Gandhi, who didn't talk for years. *If I do that, then they will have to let me go, or at least Dad will feel guilty that he fucked up my life.* But curiosity killed my strike, and I broke my silence after several seconds.

"How long will I be here?" I demanded. Then there was another frightening pause, and finally Miss Fawn stepped in.

"Well, Abby, you shouldn't focus on that right now. Just work on your recovery."

Recovery? I'm not crazy. I'm fucking normal! What is this shit? I hadn't been this angry for a while and now I remembered how unfair this all seemed. I wanted to kill my dad. I wanted to kill this hippie chick that was standing here telling me to work on my "recovery," but instead I just sat there fuming. I decided to go back on my Gandhi strike. *I am just going to sit here and not say one fucking word.*

"Well," continued Miss Fawn, "You'll be on STU for up to three months and in the Cabins for up to ten months, but this all depends on you. You might leave in thirteen months total."

I couldn't stand it anymore.

"You're talking about my recovery? Recovery from what, you assholes?" I screamed into the phone. "You're trying to tell me that I'm insane like Elizabeth just because you can't handle raising me?"

All I could hear was Dad's heavy breathing, as if he was struggling to get to the surface of a deep dive and could only swallow gulps of water. I put my head in my hands with the phone to my ear and sobbed. Part of me just wanted to hang up the phone so he couldn't hear, the other part wanted him to hear me so he could know just how much he had fucked me up.

Elizabeth is my older sister and the family freak. She was born with autism, like the guy from *Rain Man* but not as bad. When she was eighteen, she had a kind of schizophrenic breakdown. Then Mom kicked her out and Elizabeth went all over the place trying to be cured. Now I was in a recovery place exactly like where she went. I started to wonder if maybe she wasn't so fucked up, or whether I was more fucked up than I thought. Or, if my parents just *thought* we were both fucked up as an excuse to get rid of us.

Thirteen months! I thought about how much time that was, and how much I could achieve in the real world. *God, I could have a baby in nine months. If only I had fucked Matt that night. If only I hadn't saved my virginity.* For the first time in my life, I wished I was pregnant because it would have been a way out of this place. *I'm having these thoughts from being around fucking prostitutes all day.* It so wasn't me to be actually thinking like this. *These fuckers are driving me to this.*

Though in reality, I probably wouldn't have done it. But now I was desperate. *Anything to get out of this place. Anything.*

The rest of Family Therapy was spent with me too angry and choked up to talk, and Miss Fawn doing all the talking. My dad didn't say much. She acted like this place was a good thing. I wanted her to take off her hippie sandals and step into my fucking shoes. *I bet one minute upstairs and that hyperactive hippie would be changing her attitude.*

After I hung up the phone, Miss Fawn told me that if I made out a contract and got out of the hospital robe, they might let me go out to the Cabins. Good. Because then I could kill my family.

Before I left, I asked Miss Fawn if I would have Family Therapy with my mom, too. She gave me a look of complete confusion. "We'll talk about it during another Family Therapy," she said nervously. Good. Now she was the one uncomfortable and uncertain.

When I got back to STU, I held up my hand and asked to fill out one of those contracts, so I could get into the blue clothes called scrubs. Miss Curran smiled.

"I'll have you meet with Dannie. She'll show you how to fill them out."

I wondered what kind of person Miss Curran was when she went home. Did her whole personality change? Was she married? Kids of her own? Even when she was a bitch, I still saw her as a nice person in the real world. Miss Blankered probably was not.

I went back to my bed and sat there waiting to meet Dannie the Dyke. She was so masculine looking, the closest thing to a boy that was up here. Unfortunately she wasn't my type.

As we sat in the Day Room, I imagined what my friends would think about all of this. They would tell me of their many adventures and ask, "What did you do for the past year, Abby?" And I would tell them, "I just sat on a fucking bed. But sometimes

I got to sit in chairs that were circled, and once, I even sat in them when they were in two circles."

Dannie sat down next to me. I felt uncomfortable with her being so close, and had never been so pleased with the Staff members as when they asked her to move over because she was "breaking my boundaries."

Breaking my boundaries. I liked the sound of that. I had never heard of that one before. We both just sat there, looking at each other awkwardly, knowing if we talked, we would get in some serious shit for breaking a rule, so we played it safe; we just sat there.

Miss Blankered finally stepped in. "You girls can talk now. I'm aware of your conversation." She said this like she was God reciting a commandment. She spun total control. It made me sick.

"Hey, Abby," Dannie said with a goofy, overexcited expression on her chubby face. She reminded me of an enormous Cabbage Patch doll, only she was the boy kind. Dannie had a piece of paper clenched in her fat fists. It was written in markers and looked as though a kid had scribbled on it.

"Hi, Dannie," I said, wishing I could talk to Rochelle instead. She would be a whole lot more interesting, and I wouldn't fear her looking up my hospital robe.

"I made personal goals to try and reach," she said, pointing to a piece of paper, "And you have to do the same thing. You make up your own goals. My first goals were Group goals. I would call five Expression Groups and three Confront Groups."

Expression Groups were groups where you had to talk about your feelings. Confront Groups were basically tattle-telling on someone for big things (like talking in any way), little things (like not flushing the toilet), or stupid things (like not taking hair out of your brush). I usually got a lot of Confront Groups called on me. There was a whole procedure. Someone would call a Confront Group then

I would have to say, "I accept your Confront," since I always had done something. Then in Group, we voted on a Consequence.

I fucking hated Confront and Expression Groups. Both were ways of either getting other people in trouble, or saying stupid things to the Group. It all seemed totally pointless. But I needed some goals here.

Things were easy for me when it came to Consequences because I was on Suicide Precautions, which made moving around the unit virtually impossible. I couldn't do half my Consequences. Like, I couldn't clean anything because cleaning fluids could be dangerous. So all I did was make announcements, or write pages of apologies with a crayon.

Dannie then pointed to the next set of goals, which were Group Therapy ones. "You have to call time in Group, and have set issues to talk about. If you do this, you'll fulfill your goals," Dannie explained.

I thought about this one very carefully. I fucking hated talking in Group. It reminded me of being convicted of my crimes a hundred times over by the freaks who did much worse. But I started to work on my scrub contract. I wrote exactly what Dannie did, I just copied from her, and the Staff accepted my proposal. Over the next two days, I had to call my Groups and talk in them. I dreaded a whole two days of this.

TIME: 1:20 pm   **PATIENT NAME: Abigail Vona**

Group Treatment note: Patient stated "I don't want my parents to come up. I want them to want to come up. I feel like it will bother my progress. I don't want to bring it up because it will be like me asking them to see if they really care because I don't believe they do."

- Dr. K. Wisely

Day 15

For the first time in my life, I actually looked for someone to tattle on. I felt like a cop. I wanted to tell on Amy because she liked to tell on me. Sometimes, I think she made things up, but she had been here for what seemed like forever and knew all the fucking rules upside down. She was also a total perfectionist, taking the time to do every thing right, so there was nothing to tattle on with her.

It was frustrating, everyone I wanted to tell on, I couldn't, because they knew how to act. So, I settled for the new girl who everyone thought was a liar, Saint Mary.

I told on Mary for not throwing away her juice cup from lunch, and then Confronted her for eating before the moment of silence. I even told on her for not telling anyone that the toilet paper needed changing. To my surprise, I liked calling Confront Groups. It gave me something to do, and I felt important in a petty way.

TIME: 9:47 pm   **PATIENT NAME: Abigail Vona**

Milieu Treatment note: Patient seems unaware and self-absorbed. Patient seems to pay little attention to what is being said. Patient seems to have some hostility towards another patient.

- R. Curran

Chapter -5

PLAYING DRESS UP

Day 17

I was staring at the purple dots in the industrial-strength rug under my bed when the buzzer sounded loud and clear.

Miss Curran and Miss Blankered looked at each other. "Coyote Clan," said Miss Curran. "I'll go."

Ten minutes later, the door flung open with screams.

"Trusted Area! Trusted Area!" yelled Amy, and all the girls ran to their beds in the back. I just sat there spellbound, staring at the chaos. I didn't know what "Trusted Area" meant or why the girls were running there. While they ran to the back of the room, nine Staff carried in a hysterical black girl. I don't think I had ever seen all of the Staff in the same place at one time. Some faces I recognized, others I didn't.

The girl was struggling, but they held her tightly in a blanket like an oversized burrito, keeping her arms and legs still so she could only wiggle her midsection, fish-like. The blanket was bound around her, preventing her from hurting herself or the Staff. She was shrieking and spitting everywhere, and said "fuck" more times than I could count. To me, this seemed foreign until I realized I had once been that screaming, swearing, spitting girl.

I didn't want to move, I had a front row seat. The Staff wrestled the girl down to the floor, right beside me. Some of them stared at me and I heard Miss Curran, "Go to the Trusted Area, Abby, now!"

I snapped back to myself, feeling supercharged and free for the ten yards I sprinted. I hadn't run in such a long time, and it felt good to stretch my legs. I ran to the Trusted Area, which turned out to be two beds in the back, hidden from the Staff's constant surveillance. These beds were for the two most trusted girls. This was my first time there. The whole Group sat in a circle.

All the girls sat with their heads against their legs except Mary. Her eyes grew bright watching the black girl fight all the Staff. She kept whispering to the other girls but nobody listened to her. I really wanted to talk too, but I decided to tell on her instead because I wanted to fulfill my goals and get into my scrubs. Amy stared at Mary. I knew she would tattle, but this time I wanted to beat her to it.

Was the Staff worried about all of us planning a rebellion if we talked? I imagined Rochelle teaming up with Mary, and knew this wasn't far from impossible.

"Get the fuck off!" the black girl said for the hundredth time. "You're squishing my boob!"

Some girls were crying. *Did they know the girl?* To me, this was exciting. It was the only real entertainment we had had on the unit, except maybe Rochelle's prostitution stories.

We sat like rounded balls for about twenty minutes. When the screaming calmed down I heard footsteps approach us.

Mary quickly put her head down.

"Y'all right?" said a heavy-set woman with long brown pigtails. Though a very plain woman, she had a cowboy cool, like Clint Eastwood. I had seen her pass the window before with a Group of girls.

Suddenly, I remembered Mary. *Maybe if I tell on her I'll be able to go to the Cabins early, because of my honesty.* My hand shot up.

"Yes?" the husky woman asked.

"May I make a Confront?"

The woman gave a sly smile.

"No, but you can tell me, and I'll tell your Staff." She seemed amused.

"Well," I started, "Mary was talking when all of us had our heads down."

As soon as I said this, Mary gave a look as if she hadn't done it, but the rest of the Group murmured that they had heard it too.

"Which of these lovely ladies is Mary?"

I pointed to Mary's bed where she sat ready to argue. The woman nodded and then told us to continue putting our heads down. I knew the woman wouldn't forget to tell the Staff for me. She seemed strong and smart and I trusted her. The black girl finally stopped screaming so they moved her to the kennel room. She bawled hysterically all night long until I fell asleep. When I woke up, she was gone.

TIME: 1:26 pm   **PATIENT NAME: Abigail Vona**

Group Treatment note: Patient stated, "I always wanted superficial things like a Corvette, a cell phone, or a hair dryer. When I got what I wanted, I'd want something else. It gave me joy to get these things. I get jealous of my friends who have more than me. I'm scared to grow up. I've never felt complete. One of the staff said she hates people like me and I look up to her because she is so solid. I wish I could be like her. But my mother thinks what makes a person is what they have." Patient made no further disclosures at this time.

- Dr. K. Wisely

Day 18

"Focuses" were not just statements, or words of advice, and we knew it. They were verdicts and warnings of what we had to do, or more frightening, what would be done *to* us.

Dr. Wisely took out the next piece of paper, "Mary, you're not a saint," he started. "Welcome to the Coyote Clan!"

What? I wanted to jump up from the chair, rip the papers from his hand and stomp all over them. Precious Mary had the widest grin on her face, which only made matters worse. It made me want to scream! It was unfair, she had just arrived and now she was already leaving. She even broke the rules last night during a restraint, didn't that matter?

Dr. Wisely continued, "Rochelle, you're finally coming out of your shell, we are proud. Katherine? Talk about happier—"

Suddenly, the door flew open, interrupting Dr. Wisely. I knew the drill this time and ran for the Trusted Area. I only got a glimpse, but it was the same girl.

"Bring it on, you fucks! Bring it on!" she yelled. "If there were more of me, I'd fuck you the fuck up!"

She didn't ask them to get off. It was almost like she was taunting them. She went on for hours. There would be periods of quiet then she would start it up all over again.

Unlike the day before when she pleaded, cried and apologized, this time the girl fell asleep fighting and somehow ended up in the bed next to mine. All night the Staff walked around her bed, giving me no peace or time to sleep. I knew I'd be staring at clocks all day. I really wanted to go back to sleep to avoid punishment, but this was definitely more interesting.

TIME: 7:05 am   **PATIENT NAME: Abigail Vona**

Milieu Treatment note: Patient seemed to be having problems sleeping throughout the night and sitting up and watching the clock. Tossing and turning periodically. Patient appeared dazed and confused. Patient remains in gowns for being a threat to herself.

- R. Curran

Day 19

This time the black girl was still there in the morning. During pill-time, I got the chance to have a closer look at her. She was about sixteen with a body that reminded me of a young racehorse. She was pretty, with a crazed bewildered look that intimidated me. And by the look on Amy's face, I wasn't the only one intimidated.

The pill lady called her Shakira and handed her a wide assortment of brightly colored pills that she struggled to swallow.

Shakira did everything we did throughout the morning, and I wondered if she would stay. She walked around the unit with her hair sticking up in every direction. Nobody wanted to look at her for fear of getting seriously hurt.

Miss Curran called for our attention. "As you can see girls, Shakira is part of our Group. She is readjusting her meds, and needs your support until she is ready to go back out to the Cabins."

Things had suddenly become more interesting. I hoped there might be a revolt, and that I might finally be able to escape this place. I wondered if the Staff felt nervous around Shakira like Amy and I did. I sort of admired them all for their bravery, though I still hated their fucking guts.

Shakira sat on her bed with the rest of us, glaring daggers. She reminded me of a crazy African witch who was cursing us all in her head.

"Dannie," said Miss Curran, who had taken over Group Therapy that day, "talk more in Group about your anger please."

Dannie's face reddened with anger from the Focus itself.

"Abby!" My stomach jumped. *Please let me go to the Cabins.* "You haven't been helping yourself to get off Suicide Precautions. When we look at your life, you remind us of a little girl playing dress up." Her voice vibrated through my body. "You never have any responsibility, nor do you take responsibility for yourself or your actions. You float around expecting everything to be done for you." By now I was cringing, dreading the thought of looking up and seeing the whole Group staring back at me. "So," Miss Curran said, "you are now going to be Group Leader."

What? What is that?

I heard an "aagh" like a groan from the Group. Katherine started giggling.

"Amy will explain it to you after Group," said Miss Curran, noticing my confusion. "But you know one of your duties is to start Group, right?"

"Yeah," I said. *Usually Amy starts Group. They gave me her job. Why? There's got to be a catch.* A rollercoaster of thoughts careened through my head. I had never asked or even bothered to think about why Amy started all of these Groups. But the thing about being a little girl playing dress up? I mean, I wasn't really like a little girl, I just never took interest in having any responsibility. I was fine doing just what they told me to do. I wanted to be independent, not fucking bossing everyone around.

Fuck Miss Curran, I was clearing my throat before I could even think, "I'm not going to talk about the runaway," I stated.

"So, you admit it was a runaway?" asked Amy, smirking.

You bitch. You always have to talk don't you? It was enough that I had told them what I'd done. Was it so necessary to put a label on it? This is exactly what I wanted to say to them, but the words couldn't come out of my mouth. So I just said "Yes" for the sake of not arguing. I tried to ignore Amy. "I probably should never have done it, and I feel really bad. I mean, I should have at least asked my dad." This would have to be the most insincere thing I have ever said in my entire life. I didn't regret it, not at all.

"You really don't sound convincing, Abby," Katherine said, staring at me with her depressing little eyes.

Well I'm sorry I don't have a thousand issues like you, you little shit. At least I'm not a sick little girl whose only enjoyment in life is slicing her wrists whenever she passes by a sharp object. I decided to give up talking, I had tried with them. "Who else calls time?" I asked.

The whole Group put up their hands, but my decision had already been made on our new guest, Shakira. How could I resist?

Shakira took a deep breath and half pulled herself up from her slouch. Rochelle watched her every move, and within seconds followed her and adopted the same body language. I had noticed it from the day before. It was almost a joke. Shakira and Rochelle both lounged in their chairs with an "I don't give a fuck" look. Rochelle had recently stopped giving off the impression of being a gangster, after she had been on the unit for a while. It was strange to see her go back to her old self so easily. Rochelle just wanted to remind us that she could play the tough black girl.

Rochelle and Shakira may have seemed the same, but they weren't — they were like two different kinds of snakes with the same markings. The first snake's fangs can kill you, but the other snake that looks the same can't defend itself against predators. Of course the safe snake is still feared because it looks dangerous. Rochelle took on the characteristics of people she feared and even of those who fucked with her, but she wasn't dangerous herself.

Shakira, on the other hand, was poison. She went to extremes, hated authority, had an anger problem, and was a natural born leader who didn't take anybody's shit. She had a lot of pride and was overly strong-willed.

Shakira was a "state" kid and Rochelle was "paying," which surprised me at first, because Rochelle's mother was poor. Later I learned she had a rich aunt.

At The Village, there were three types of kids: "state," "court," and "paying." "State" kids were the responsibility of the state of Tennessee and had usually lived in foster homes or were adopted, but there was some big problem with the kids or the "placement." For state kids, going anywhere or leaving anywhere did not matter, they had been doing it all their lives, they were usually immune to anything. "Court" kids had real parents, but they had been arrested, and instead of going to jail, they were sent here and the state paid for it — Dannie and Mary were court kids. And then there were "paying" like Katherine and me. Usually these were kids from out of state whose parents thought they were problems and had enough money to send them here.

"Well, first," said Shakira, " I would like to apologize to y'all." She didn't seem very fake in her apology. Her facial expressions changed dramatically from *don't fuck with* me to *I'm sorry* in a matter of seconds.

"Last night, I flipped out and was real angry. Not at The Village okay? But at my mom and my meds . . . " She trailed off, looking as though she was about to cry.

"See, no one here knows me besides Amy and the Staff, so I feel kind of weird telling y'all this, but my mom . . . she never does nothin' for me, and she skipped therapy again yesterday." Shakira clenched the arm of her chair and she looked very upset.

Miss Curran nodded, sympathetic to Shakira's pain. It was

nice to see them both being honest.

"Well, Shakira, you know this already, and you need to move on with your life."

Shakira responded to this with a look of absolute hate, which turned to sadness, followed by tears. Shakira wiped them away on her shirt and then looked pissed off again, as though she was a child who had just been caught doing something naughty. I guess Shakira was too cool to cry, and us catching her out made her even more mad. She could barely speak.

"It's not all my mom," she stammered. "I mean, I'm so fucked-up in the head," she said, getting all worked up again. "And my clan, they're on 'Shut Down.'"

I started to like this girl. She was real. Not like some of the other attention-starved brats in this place.

"Well, y'all don't know," Shakira continued, "but I'm a Coyote, and I love my clan. They's my people." She sounded like a cave woman and even pounded her chest. I had to suck in my cheeks to hide a smile.

She went on without looking at anyone, just staring at the ground. Rochelle stared at her like a wolf, watching her every move and ready to copy her.

Shakira went on, her whole body shaking with the sound of her voice. "Well, when I got restrained, it was my first in two months, right?" She said this as though being restrained for her was an everyday thing.

"See, I sort of like to get restrained. It gets out my anger. I'm a very physical person." I couldn't believe what I was hearing. *Being restrained was, without a doubt, the single worst experience I ever had in my life.* I thought she was fucking crazy. It made me think of Katherine and her cutting. *How could anybody get off on hurting themselves in order to make themselves feel better?*

"Sometimes, I get so much anger inside I feel like I'm about to explode."

She made a gesture with her fist, forcing me to imagine her killing someone.

I looked at Mary. She would be going out to the Coyote Clan in less than a week. She was going to have to live with people like Shakira. Oh, I was happy about that.

TIME: 10:27 pm   **PATIENT NAME: Abigail Vona**

Group Treatment note: Patient stated, "I want attention but I can't really handle it. I don't know what to do. I feel strange, nervous. I'm not used to people noticing me. The whole day I've felt uncomfortable. I feel scared now because staff is asking me how I feel." Patient seemed attentive and offered nothing further.

- Dr. K. Wisely

Day 20

I was sitting on my bed when one of the Staff handed me a piece of paper and told me to go to the Day Room, all of eight feet away, to meet Amy so we could talk about my new responsibilities. On the paper was a schedule:

6:45: Rise. Make beds.

7:00: Exercise.

7:30: Breakfast.

8:15: Clean up.

8:25: Silent time.

11:30: Lunch.

12:15: Clean up.

12:25: Group Therapy.
13:30: Silent time.
17:30: Dinner.
18:10: Clean up.
18:20: Showers.
19:45: Silent time.
21:10: Bed.

Maybe I could use my dyslexia as an excuse not to do any of this. I did it all the time. Other kids hated me for it. It was definitely my "get out of jail free" card. And when a teacher gave me a hard time, I would call her ignorant for not knowing that "a dyslexic is a very special person." In fact, I did the same thing here.

Twice a week for part of the day we had "school." They had a woman come in who gave us packets of math or English or whatever, depending on our grade level. We would read the papers or try to do the problems. No one took it seriously, I mean they never even gave us real books. And I explained to the teacher that I was dyslexic so she gave me stuff but didn't bother me much. But I decided not to use this strategy with Staff, for now.

The Staff had me sit next to Amy and reminded us that they were aware of our conversation. They sounded like machines when they said this. I hated Amy more than ever and didn't want to be around her. Everything was an act with her. Whenever I saw her, all I could think of were these really weird visions of her molesting children. She reminded me of my sister and her insanity, only Amy seemed sneakier. I'm sure she thought about touching me or the other girls. I mean, we were all locked up in this place together — somebody had to be thinking about it. Well, probably Dannie more than anyone — I would tiptoe past her sometimes, making myself paranoid at what sleazy images were running through her head. These girls were so fucking creepy.

"Hello, Abby," Amy sang, with an exaggerated smile, like some twisted cartoon character. I didn't want to acknowledge her, but Staff was right there.

"Hi," I said.

"Okay, I'm going to tell you about my job that you are going to do. Are you excited?" She talked to me as though I was two, and I didn't want to hear her pathetic little voice in my ear. I forced myself to say something.

"I'm a little confused on what to do."

"Well, you have to run everything, you know . . . bathroom breaks and stuff like that . . . exactly what I do," she said snottily.

Each day and all day, Amy had her hand in the air and was always asking if the Group could do this or that. I never paid much attention, I now regretted not watching her every move.

"Don't worry, I'll guide you today."

I had to stand next to Amy the whole day. There was so much stuff to memorize. I didn't know how there could be so many rules for such a small room. *They make things confusing here on purpose so we can go even more out of our minds.*

I sat on my bed and thought about my Focus. *You remind us of a little girl playing dress up with no responsibilities whatsoever.* Hearing that was like a hard slap across the face — it burned. I never had any responsibilities or boundaries at home. My dad was always giving me whatever I wanted, and let me do whatever I goddamn pleased. I never had a job or anything, not even a curfew. I even went to the finest schools for underachieving dyslexic slackers. Before I knew it, I thought that was the life. But thinking about it in STU, I didn't know if that was the best thing for me, even though it had been kind of fun.

TIME: 2:30 pm   **PATIENT NAME: Abigail Vona**

Milieu Treatment Note: Problem #1 (Depressive Disorder) Patient finally expressed herself saying "I am trying to figure out what's wrong with me. I've always had trouble at times with spelling, words, etc. I've gone years with my teachers giving me tapes so I didn't have to read. I really am trying in here, I just keep messing up." Patient was tearful and seemed sincere.

- R. Curran

Chapter -4

KILL

Day 21

Gigantic hands shook me. "Wake up! Wake up!" the woman yapped, "Time to call bathroom break!" The night Staff was even less charming than the day Staff.

At first I didn't comprehend, then it hit me. Unlike Amy, I had real trouble performing the role of Group Leader. All morning I had trouble remembering the little questions I had to ask. Fortunately, the Staff guided me, like a toddler helped by a mother during her first steps. I was helpless. I was hopeless. I was used to having people doing things for me all the time.

At first, the Staff made things very easy. They would say, "Ask us if you can make your bed," and I did. But a simple thing like running people in and out of the bathroom to brush their teeth was an entire list of about twelve questions that were impossible to remember. I was allowed only a sheet of paper with an outline, most of it had to come from memory.

I didn't see the reason for me being Group Leader other than to make a point that I was a brat with nothing really stable in my life.

As much as I hated having Amy's obnoxious voice ordering me around, it was far better than me messing things up. Because of my slowness and inability to run things, we were late for everything, even when the Staff constantly prompted me. Everything took even longer because the Staff waited until I asked them what I was supposed to ask them, instead of just asking me to ask.

After lunch on our beds, I lined up the Group to throw away their trash. I asked the question for them to get in line. But then my mind went blank. This was when Staff would tell me what to do. Instead, the Staff ignored me. I raised my hand and asked them what to ask. The Group stood there with food in their hands, waiting for permission to throw it out. Minutes passed. The whole thing just seemed so stupid. It didn't help that Shakira was glaring at me the whole time, making me feel cornered and stupid.

Finally Miss Blankered called on me.

"Miss Blankered, may you please tell me what I need to ask next?"

But Miss Blankered pretended she didn't hear me. *This is a conspiracy.* The entire room fell deathly silent. The Group stood before me like *Dawn of the Dead* people, throwing me angry looks and rolling their eyes in frustration. I started panicking. I was sinking into a swamp. My face flushed red. I wanted to cuss out the entire fucking Staff.

I quickly thought of ways I could get the Staff to give in so they could tell me what to do. *They have to.* I couldn't do this on my own. I wasn't nearly as smart as Amy. *Maybe if I just stand here, they'll get tired of looking at me and have Amy go back as leader. That's what they'll do, they'll put her back as leader.*

I made desperate attempts to provoke pity from the Staff but we just stood there with our food. Then Shakira took a bite of banana she was about to throw out. The whole Group looked at her as if she was insane — no one was so stupid as to eat after the Staff told them not to. And she did it right in front of Miss Curran. That really took some guts. Shakira even gave Miss Curran a little smirk. And Miss Curran acted like she didn't even notice!

Amy's hand shot up in the air to Confront Shakira. But Miss Curran wouldn't notice her hand, either. All three Staff just stared back, focusing on me. It became unbearable. I had no choice but to just try and guess the questions I had to ask. One thing I knew was my questions always had to start with "may" and "please."

"Please, may the Group throw away their trash?" I asked in a wavering voice.

Miss Curran cocked her head. "Wouldn't that be disorganized if they all went up at once to throw their trash away?"

I remembered we had to go up in the order from most trustworthy to the least. I must have rephrased the question about ten times before I finally got it right.

The Group finally got to throw their food in the trash. I wanted to kill the entire ward. The Staff was stupid, and southern, and didn't understand that I was learning disabled. I am dyslexic! In other words, I had a fucked up mind and couldn't do shit that others could do! Fucking idiots!

TIME: 4:30 pm   **PATIENT NAME: Abigail Vona**

Milieu Treatment note: Patient appears to be a poor leader. Patient seems to act confused more often. Patient earns more Consequences and seems to want to blame it on her being "dumb." It is unclear at this time what is an act and what the patient just does not understand.

                                                                    -J. Blankered

Day 23

During the week, I started to memorize the questions I had to ask. In Group, everyone complained about how frustrated they were with me. So I was determined to make it more difficult for everyone to blame me. I got the Group to all of our meetings and activities on time. The whole thing became entertaining, and at least it gave me something to do. Better than sitting on my damn bed. Amy, however, hated not having the job. When the Staff didn't look, she would give me these mean-ass looks. Yeah, well too bad, bitch.

That I was still on Suicide Precautions really bothered me. I didn't want to die, couldn't these people take a joke? It was hard to work myself out of a hole that I was never really in to begin with. I was just about to give up and start to do my silent Gandhi thing again, when Miss Curran came up to me and said, "No more Suicide Precautions for you, Abby. And, you earned your scrubs." I looked at her like she had lost her mind and then I just wanted to jump up and hug her. She was by far my favorite Staff. Miss Curran looked genuinely happy for me. This meant real food! This was one step closer to being home, one step closer to my freedom.

During lunch, Miss Curran asked if I wanted to pass out food. She usually gave this job to Amy, but since I was off Suicide Precautions, she had me do it to celebrate. Passing out food was the greatest. I was able to walk around the unit, taking in every little detail and could even control who got what and how much. I gave myself three extra sugar packets and was tempted to take an extra pastry, but Staff were watching me like hawks. I was even allowed back in the Trusted Area to give Amy her napkin.

When I walked in there, I didn't like what I saw. Amy was rocking back and forth with a possessed look on her face. I gave her the napkin and quickly left. I couldn't run without Staff fearing that I was trying to escape. Two minutes later, I heard Amy's voice asking if she could call a Confront Group.

"Group!" she blurted. "I Confront Abby for interacting."

I looked at her in awe. I hadn't said a word to her. *What is she talking about?*

"What did she say, Amy?" Miss Curran asked, surprised.

Amy's expression was serious and contrasted with mine. I gave a nervous laugh. One of my personality flaws is laughing under stress.

"Well," Amy went on, "she said, 'I hate this place.'"

My jaw hit the floor. *Why would I say that when I was in a good mood?* Miss Curran noticed this, and unlike other confrontations for interacting, she dismissed it instead of sending me to the corner to stare at the wall.

I had never felt so angry and hurt. *How could anyone be so crazy?* I went back to my bed. My good mood turned bad. Then I started to lose it and cry. Three weeks ago, I wouldn't have given a shit about something like this, but now it really affected me. I raised my hand.

Miss Curran called on me, "Yes, Abby?"

"Could I speak with you . . . in private?" I sniffled, wiping my nose on my sleeve like a four-year-old.

"Of course, Abby, come over."

I went right over. I felt comfortable with Miss Curran. She was what I wanted my mom to be like.

"Miss Curran, I didn't say anything. I don't know what she's talking about. Why would she lie like that?" I got it out between sobs.

"It's okay. I know that, Abby. I could tell that nothing had happened," Miss Curran said gently. I really loved Miss Curran at that moment, but wondered why she didn't punish Amy immediately.

Then it hit me. *Could Amy be schizophrenic?* I suggested this to Miss Curran but she just laughed sweetly and told me to go back to bed.

People accusing me of shit that had never happened and thinking I was saying stuff to them when I hadn't was not a new thing for me to deal with. My sister was paranoid and schizophrenic that way.

When I was little, I got along with my sister, Elizabeth, and followed her example, which was a bad thing. She is eleven years older than I am. I can remember she would babysit me, and we would do weird things. At the time I didn't know any better. We would run around the neighborhood naked or we would act like vampires, but very evil vampires, not Halloween vampires. Then she would order pornography on television, pay-per-view, and just sit there and watch it and make me sit there and watch it too. She would also get horror movies. She was obsessed by horror movies, the most awful gory horror movies. By the time I was five years old, I think I had seen enough pornography and horror movies to last a lifetime.

When I got a little older, Elizabeth started to hear voices. Sometimes she thought I was out to hurt her, even though I was a kid. She became crazy and violent. I remember she pushed me down the stairs because she heard voices and thought I was trying to kill her. My mom found me at the bottom of the steps hurt and crying. She went to my sister's room and threw her radio off the balcony, breaking it. "If you're going to hurt your sister, you won't get away with it!" my mom yelled. I felt bad for my sister at the time, her radio was her life and only friend, and it was smashed completely.

Amy wasn't like my sister, though; my sister couldn't help how she acted. And Amy didn't have the problems my sister did, even though she had beaten up her own little sister. What worried me more was that being in this place, maybe I was the one becoming like my sister. That truly scared me.

TIME: 3:25 pm   **PATIENT NAME: Abigail Vona**

Group Treatment note: Patient expressed "My mother and I took makeup from my sister and never told her. I'd say 'she never uses it, and doesn't know how to put it on.' "

- Dr. K. Wisely

Day 24

I got a letter from my mom. It was the first letter I got from anyone. My dad hadn't written me because we were having therapy together. And even if my friends had my address, The Village would probably block the mail. The letter had already been opened. It didn't shock me that Staff went through the letters here, because there was no privacy in the first place.

The letter was in cursive writing and I found it hard to tell the difference between her handwriting and my dyslexia.

My mother lost custody of me years ago, but my dad had me live with her when he got tired of me. I guess she always had a way to make me feel as though I was wanted.

Dear Abby,

I hope it was the right decision to send you there and I'm glad your father went along with it. I just hope that you're doing well and making something out of yourself. The way you and your brother were living at his house wasn't the right way to grow up because you had no guidance there. I guess I know how you must feel sweetheart. Just know this is not your fault. If you were living with me, this would have never happened. I know that you are angry with your brother too for not being there. I actually agree with you, but you know very well that your father is afraid of Ted. All the times when Ted stole from you, your father did nothing about it. That would have never happened at my house. Your father could have prevented all of this, but he still doesn't face his problems. I hope someday you will see that being there is a good thing and soon you will be able to help yourself. I promise you this is for the best.

Love you more than you know,
Mom

Mom was right. *My fucking brother should be here, and my dad is a spineless prick.* It was enough to get me started all over again. I sat on my bed and sulked.

TIME: 8:07 pm   **PATIENT NAME: Abigail Vona**

Group Treatment note: Patient expressed "There was a time I was happy. I felt alone with my dad. I had friends over and smoked weed. I'd go places without telling him. He called the cops, and got me sent here. I stole a lot. I threw things. I feel like a spoiled brat." Patient seemed to make excuses for herself and appeared to blame others. Patient seemed to not know how to take responsibility for herself.

- Dr. K. Wisely

Day 26

I rounded up the Group for therapy. I was actually a pretty good Group Leader now.

Shakira hadn't been joining any of the Group meetings, she was always in bed. Maybe she had not adjusted to her meds. Actually, the rest of us weren't very different from her, we just sat on our beds all day. Just then, Shakira screamed out a "fuck you!" from her bed. Then she went back to sleep.

Dr. Wisely started to read off the Focuses, like Shakira's swearing was nothing more than a birdcall.

"Abby, you've been doing very well. We know that you have more to talk about than you probably admit to yourself. We'll help you with a subject. Let's start with your mother."

I gulped hard, almost choking on my own spit. *They want me to talk about my mom and not my brother? Did nothing in this freakhouse make any sense? Did these fuckers even read my mom's letter?*

My shit-head of a brother is the problem here, not my mom.

Dr. Wisely went on, "Rochelle, you have begun to talk about your prostitution. But tell us about how you felt, more than war stories this time. There's a fine line between pride and shame."

A fine line between pride and shame. I never really thought about that before, but it was very clear in Rochelle's case. She either felt pride for her many adventures or ashamed about fucking so many guys.

Amy received the exact same focus as the last time about how she acted at home versus STU, Katherine had to talk about "happy" memories, Dannie had to describe her anger towards her family. Talk about predictable shit.

When it was my turn to speak, Dr. Wisely interrupted me, "Hang on there, Abby." He peered at me through the small frames of his glasses. "The Group knows nothing of your mother. Do you mind shedding some light on the topic?"

I stared back at him. "Well, my mom has really bad mood swings but normally she's really nice, when she wants to be. Nice when she's having a good day, but hell-scary when she's angry. When she's angry, she's like a bulldozer. Funny you mention her, because she wrote me a letter the other day." I knew he knew about the letter and wanted me to talk about it.

Dr. Wisely nodded in approval. "What did it say?"

"She talked about my brother, Ted, and how he should be here too, which is so true. He is a lot worse than I am. He smoked me up for the first time, and he gets really bad grades. Only difference is, he's a boy. He's sneaky and when he does get caught, my dad, like, totally believes him. Like the time he locked me out of the house and I had to call the cops to get back in. These cops went through his room and stumbled on a lot of pipes and pot. Well, the cops then had a meeting with my dad and get this — my dad believes my brother."

I was suddenly on a roll, and wanted to tell them more stuff, but Dr. Wisely butted in.

"So . . . why do you think your mom told you this, Abby? I do believe you about your brother and I do wish he were here. But we are working with you. Blaming him won't get you anywhere."

I didn't see what he was getting at, and my time was up. I called on Dannie who talked in detail about how she beat her little brothers and then had a fit and hurt her mother. She didn't want to do those things again. I pictured her family as total trailer-trash hicks who married their sisters. Dannie looked inbred. With her male body and deep voice I thought it was ironic they named her Dannie. Maybe her parents couldn't figure out her sex. Or maybe she was one of those he-she hermaphrodites.

But, unlike me, Dannie's shame was very believable and it didn't seem like lies to get her out of STU, even though she told us she wanted to leave and be with her family. Her family had called the cops because her anger got so out of control. She was sent to The Village by the court after her arrest. I wondered why she never beat the Staff or got restrained. Dannie then called on Rochelle, who had gone back to her pouty face.

"Well, I want to talk about my Focus. I don't really understand it. Do you want me to talk about my experiences or not? I just don't get it."

Nobody answered her, and finally Dr. Wisely stepped in, "Well Rochelle, just don't brag."

She pouted some more, "What do you mean, 'there is a fine line between bragging and shame'?"

I wanted to say something, and for the first time, I actually did. "What I get from your Focus . . ." I paused and looked around. I felt really uncomfortable. *Maybe I'm out of place saying something to Rochelle.* "Well, you seem either proud of your experiences, or ashamed of them, depending on your mood." And I wanted to add, "Who you're around affects you, too," and point out her behavior with Shakira, but I didn't.

To my surprise, Rochelle took this in and nodded her head. She understood.

TIME: 3:53 pm　　　　　　　　　**PATIENT NAME: Abigail Vona**

Group Treatment note: Abigail expressed "I was so shocked that my peers accepted me because I was not putting on an act. I was not being dingy and everything went okay." She made good, positive eye contact. "It felt good being accepted and being very real." She seemed very truthful and genuinely shocked by her peers' reactions. She seemed relieved and happy.

- Dr. K. Wisely

Day 31

I returned from Family Therapy where my father and I barely spoke. When Miss Fawn dropped me off at STU, she whispered something to Miss Curran. Five minutes later, Miss Curran gave me a piece of paper, "Miss Fawn wants you to work on a list of things to talk about in Family Therapy."

The fact I needed to make a list of things to talk about on the phone with my father was pathetic.

"You have four categories," she said, pointing to the piece of paper. "One is superficial; then your mother issues; then future issues . . ."

Getting out of here, that's my future issue.

"And the fourth is stepmother issues."

She left me with a marker and a blank piece of paper. I looked at the paper and made my four categories. The only ones I wanted to fill out were future and stepmom, but the stuff I would write might be inappropriate. All I wanted to write under stepmom was: *Bitch! She should be dead. Or she should fall down a flight of stairs or get hit by a car.*

TIME: 3:12 pm   **PATIENT NAME: Abigail Vona**

Group Treatment note: Patient expressed, "My mother wouldn't notice the things staff notices. She wouldn't care. Why would staff point things out, why would they care?" Patient seems to act as if she is very stupid so she won't have to follow rules. She acts as if she does not know all rules, when she actually does, especially rules told to her by staff. She seems unkempt in her appearance. She maintained appropriate hygiene at shower time.

-Dr. K. Wisely

Day 33

At Group, Dr. Wisely gave me my Focus. I liked Dr. Wisely, even though I knew he hated me. He was like a kind but stern grandfather. "Abby, we understand you can't relate to your father or talk to your stepmother. Is that why you rely so much on your mother's guidance?"

I got what he was saying about not being able to talk to my dad and stepmom, but couldn't work out why he was so interested in my mom.

"So Abby, why don't you start today." Dr. Wisely seemed to say this more to Amy than to me. He had given everyone a Focus but Amy. I was really confused. Why did he skip Amy's Focus?

"Dr. Wisely, Amy didn't get a Focus," I said uneasily.

"Oh, Amy doesn't need a Focus. We have been repeating it for three months. I think she can remember it."

Amy went white. She opened and closed her mouth.

"Amy, don't act like you don't know what I'm talking about," Dr. Wisely said in a tough tone. "Go on, Abby," he said, smiling at me.

Amy looked tortured and began rocking back and forth again. I kind of felt bad for her. Dr. Wisely waved his hand, gesturing for me to continue.

"Well, I call time to talk about my Focus. I understand that my dad doesn't see things and I hate my stepmom because she hates me, so it's hard for me to relate to them but the 'mom guiding me' part doesn't make sense."

Dr. Wisely nodded. "And why is that?"

"Well, we got into a fight and I haven't talked to her since."

"So before the fight, how were you?" asked Dr. Wisely, like he knew the answer already.

" Really close," I said, feeling myself missing her.

"Did she encourage you to act out against your stepmother?"

I nodded. "My mom hates my stepmother as much as I do. She supports everything that I do to her and tries her hardest to stop my stepmother from being . . ." I couldn't find a word that I could use in Group that could replace bitch, "such a bitch to us."

"Did she tell you and your brother to do anything you could to get her out of the house?" asked Dr. Wisely.

I nodded again.

"Did she tell you to try to kill her?"

"Not kill, like . . ." He was partly right. I nodded, staring straight at the floor, hating this.

"Tell me about the time you put Vaseline on the stairs so your stepmother would hurt herself. And then how you smashed her artwork."

"I was really young then. That's when my dad first got married that I did those things. I didn't really want her to die, I just wanted her to leave."

"Did your mother encourage all of this, did she tell you to do it?" asked Dr. Wisely.

"Not to do it exactly, but she thought it was pretty funny."

"Do you think that's appropriate for a mother to think this kind of thing is funny?" he asked, looking at me hard.

"I never really put much thought into it," was all I could say back to him. "My dad and I never talk. He's busy at work, and when he isn't, he's with my stepmom. My stepmom, well, I can honestly say I hate her."

Katherine stared into space then looked over at me and said, "I can totally relate. I sometimes feel all alone, and my parents don't really talk to me that much."

I continued, "Well, yesterday, I had Family Therapy, and my dad and I had nothing to say so I had to write up a list with some plans and stuff on it for the future. I can say now that I want no future with my stepmom."

"I feel sorry for you," Dannie blurted out. "I mean, though we're far from perfect, my family's so close."

I almost wanted to laugh. *Far from perfect? She beat up half her family!*

TIME: 8:39 pm   **PATIENT NAME: Abigail Vona**

Group Treatment note: Patient stated, "When I was little, my mother got in a fight with this woman. I knew a mean song and I sang it to this woman. My mother laughed and was proud of me. She thought it was creative how I stole candy. Sometimes I still think it's funny, or that people will think it's cute when I do something bad. She's a little off, my mother is. For example, stealing is right if the person is mean. Lies are okay if it's to a liar."

-Dr. K. Wisely

Chapter -3

CAT FIGHTERS

Day 34

At 10:00 am, another girl was expected. *How did they get the new ones to come in?* I imagined an airplane unloading batches of fucked-up girls in restraints, just waiting to fill empty spots. I wondered whose replacement I was and who would then replace me.

Just as I was timing girls in and out of the bathroom and making sure they came out within one minute and three seconds, I saw *it*.

I thought Staff had made a mistake, or the boys unit was full, because the new "girl" was a ten-year-old Mexican boy. No breasts or curves and crew-cut hair made *it* look about ten years old. *But that couldn't be right. Ten year olds aren't allowed here. Are they?* I spent every free moment trying to find out if, in fact, this was a boy. Whatever *it* was, *it* reminded me of a scared, cornered rat about to lash out.

At Group in the afternoon, *it* said, "Hi, my name's Veronica. I'm fourteen." Well, *she* tried to make her voice sound deeper than it was — she reminded me of a young boy going through puberty, because her voice cracked every three seconds.

She was fuckin' ugly and strange. I wondered if she would grow up to become something like the bearded lady. I looked around, and everyone was just as curious and repelled.

She smiled and gave a giggle like the Road Runner.

"I want to have my sex changed," she said. "But my adoptive mom won't let me." Still, I wondered if she wanted to be a boy or a girl.

"And I also do every drug."

"Can you name all the drugs, Veronica?" said Dr. Wisely smiling, as though not believing a word she said.

"Coke, heroin, air fresheners," she said looking up at the ceiling. She had this animated smile.

"I'm also a lesbian." *Holy fuck my question is answered.* I was wishing she would stop there, but she was just getting started.

Veronica loved attention and went on talking about all the issues she had. She had talked nearly the whole session when Dr. Wisely told her to talk tomorrow. But she had other plans.

She got up out of her chair, crossed her arms and said, "Nope!"

Two seconds later, we were in the Trusted Area, alarms going off and Veronica on the floor, screaming "fuck you" for over three hours. I was getting tired of this shit. Someone was always freaking out here.

Veronica's was by far the longest restraint. The girl didn't calm down, all you heard was "fuck," "bitch," " shit," "morons." I guess she decided this wasn't effective because she started singing nursery rhymes. "The wheels on the bus go round and round," she sang as loud as possible. This was definitely an interesting tactic but just as unsuccessful as my fake suicide screams. Veronica kept it up, "Oh Susannah, oh, don't you cry for me . . ." Then it was Christmas carols, "Deck the halls with fucking holly, la, la, la, la, la, la, la, la, la . . . "

Veronica should have burst a lung with all the noise she made.

Talk about exhausting. I had to walk by her to get to my bed. The Staff had her strapped down — arms, legs, even her forehead, nothing could move an inch. And she just kept on singing. "Jingle bells, jingle bells. . ."

I wanted to laugh but I started crying. Not because I was scared, but because I was stuck here with crazies. Maybe it was contagious and I would catch it from these girls. Then I just thought of my stepmother again because it was probably her fault I was here.

My stepmom hated me. I remembered when I first started to live with my dad. He would force the whole family to eat together — my brother, stepmom, him, and me. It was absolute hell for my brother and me. We hated being forced to eat at a table together, plus my stepmother was a terrible cook. We always made fun of her terrible food and her fat double chin behind her back. One dinner, when I reached for the chicken, she slapped my hand with a fork. It didn't really hurt that much but I used it as an excuse to call the police. Then I called my mom, who came over to yell at the bitch. My stepmom moved out of the house pretty soon after. I knew she wanted to get back at me. She was behind this! Now, I wanted to scream along with Veronica and go nuts! *Maybe that was my stepmother's plan in the first place - to have me go nuts!*

TIME: 5:46 pm   **PATIENT NAME: Abigail Vona**

Activity Time note: Patient was observed making jewelry with beads, during which she seemed somewhat isolative, but well focused. Patient seemed withdrawn but content to be in her own world. Patient seemed to wince when confronted as if only upset to get caught. Patient was compliant.

- R. Curran

Day 35

When it came time to start Group, I had something on my mind, so I launched right in: "Today, I want to talk about my stepmom." I held back a lot the temptation to scream, "The fuckin' bitch!" and go on a rampage only because I didn't feel like joining Veronica. "Well, I hate her. Honestly, I can't stand her." For some reason, no one seemed affected by my words. They just sat there looking at me blankly, like a bunch of uninhabited puppets. I wanted to get a reaction.

"She came into my life when I was seven, and was . . . I have to admit, nice, until she married my dad. After they got married, she tried to ship me out to every boarding school in other states, plus camps in the woods. She hates me. I know for a fact that she sent me here."

Amy made a strange popping noise that, along with her colorless features, made her even more alien-like. Then words came out. "Do you regret coming here?"

It was a trick question. *Of course every inch of my body regrets getting on that plane and not killing my stepmom. Maybe if I'd gotten rid of her, I would have a lesser sentence in a state prison than I would here. And I wouldn't have to deal with her when I got out.* I sat there, wondering how much of the truth I should share, or if I should lie and tell them sweetly like Amy would, "Oh, I don't regret coming here," which was the farthest thing from the truth.

"Yes, I regret it." I looked around. Amy seemed shocked. "When I was fourteen, my stepmom moved out of my dad's house, and I've only seen her twice since."

"She moved out?" asked Dannie.

Rochelle asked, "Are they still married?"

"Well, we hated each other for a year. We didn't talk, we

yelled, and one day she hit me so hard that I had to call the cops." I recalled the clear picture of her in handcuffs and held back a smile. That was a good day.

"The next day, she moved out. They're married but don't live together . . . until I go away, and then she moves back into the house, or they go on vacation together." The thought of her in my house made me sick.

Amy's puzzled expression told me she was about to ask one of her absurd questions. I was right. "How do you feel about all this?"

Fuck you, Amy. "Who else calls time? Rochelle?"

"I call time . . ." Rochelle breathed. Even her pauses held a certain suspense. "I call time to talk about getting raped." She peered at the Group's faces before going on. "I was raped three times. The first time—"

"Rochelle," Dr. Wisely interrupted, "just talk about the first one today. Don't rush it. Remember, don't talk in the third person."

Third person? I didn't know what he meant, but Rochelle seemed to understand. They must have had a private talk.

Rochelle nodded and went on. "The first time I was raped was the first time I ever had sex. I said no, but he never stopped. He just went on. It was at a party. I was thirteen. He was nineteen. He was my older cousin's friend. He was drunk. We kissed. It was the first time I ever kissed, and I told him that. I told him that was all I wanted to do, but he just went on."

Rochelle went in and out of tears as she spoke.

"Did you press charges?" asked Dr. Wisely.

Easy for him to say. It was a stupid-ass question. Cut her some fucking slack, you moron. She was a thirteen-year-old!

Rochelle puffed out her lips. "No, like I said before, he was my cousin's friend and I didn't want to cause trouble."

"Why would it cause trouble?" Katherine asked.

"Well," Rochelle sighed, "His friends went to my school—"

Dr. Wisely interrupted her again, "So, you didn't value your body enough to do something about it? Do you think that this type of thinking leads to your selling your body for sex?"

Rochelle sighed, "Yeah . . . I think so."

The room fell silent. Rochelle called on Katherine.

Katherine didn't look like she wanted to talk about her kittens today. "Miss Blankered told me to think about when I became anorexic. That was when I was young. Well, my mom, she used to tell me I needed to lose weight."

Katherine didn't seem to be lying. *Telling a little kid to lose weight?*

"Once, she lectured me on calories. I wouldn't eat much until I was eleven. Then I started to throw up. It was like releasing feelings. All my worries just went away."

Hearing this was awful. *Why would her mom say that?*

"When I was twelve, my parents sent me off to boarding school, and I would cut on myself. It just made me feel better."

Now it was Amy's turn.

"I had Family Therapy yesterday," she said, grinding her teeth. "Like always, they sat there and blamed me." Her voice shook. She seemed angry, but it was obvious that she couldn't let it out. This scared me. It was the first time she hinted at the fact that she was one angry girl, not the perfect child she pretended to be.

"My sister is doing really well. I remember when I hid the knives in weird places to get her in trouble. They thought she did it and she had gone mental. The state sent her to a hospital. Those were happy days for me. See, my family doesn't need me, my sister, she's perfect."

I looked at the clock, we were going over by five minutes but Staff didn't stop it. Seeing a glimpse of Amy's real side was very rare, like seeing bits of the moon in the day.

"At Family Therapy, when I asked to change the subject to my mom not being so strict, my dad walked out, calling me crazy. My mom's so strict. She grounded my sister for three weeks for crossing the street without permission. That's all."

The Group had never seen Amy this way. Me? Personally, I liked seeing her not so fake.

There it was, the most revealing twenty minutes I had yet encountered in here. Suddenly, I understood their problems, all of them. I may not have liked them, but they had made me understand a little.

As much as I hated this place, I was growing some kind of like for it. I remember Amy talking about this before. I thought, *she must be joking*. Now I kind of understood what she meant.

TIME: 3:25 pm   PATIENT NAME: Abigail Vona

Group Treatment note: Patient expressed feeling "kinda good." Patient stated, "I was unaware earlier. I say 'I don't get it' to avoid problems with rules. It's the easy way out to look dumb." Patient seemed to struggle with being direct.

- Dr. K. Wisely

Day 57

Back on my bed, my thoughts were distracted by Veronica, who was stretching out like a scrawny rat on her bed. The whole Group looked intently at her, waiting for her to flip out, ready to run to the Trusted Area. But she just sat there and ate her leftover lunch that Staff kept at her bed. Veronica wasn't the only one who had the luxury of sleeping in. Shakira did too. I wasn't jealous.

They would probably never see the light of day and be stuck here forever. I was surprised Shakira was so well behaved but I knew she would probably try to do something crazy.

After Veronica finished her food, she lay back down. "Get up!" said Miss Curran and Miss Blankered.

"Why? She gets to sleep, and you don't care!" Veronica said, pointing at Shakira and making things worse.

"It doesn't matter," Miss Curran said. To my surprise, Veronica slouched back down and bent against a pillow, glaring at Shakira, who was now awake and glaring at Veronica with a triumphant smile on her face.

"Don't smile at me!" Veronica said, bobbing her head up to one side and then the other.

Shakira sat right up and shot Veronica a death stare. "What you going to do, you fucking dyke? Fight me?"

Veronica jumped to her feet, breaking one of the golden rules — *do not get off your bed without permission, otherwise you get restrained.* But Shakira did the same, and a second later, they were headed right for each other to fight but Staff got between them. Miss Curran and Miss Blankered took Veronica to the ground. But they had lots of trouble with Shakira. They finally succeeded tackling her. She hit the floor with a bang.

Buzzers rang and Staff came running, as we huddled in the Trusted Area. Some of the girls were crying. I was laughing.

"Come on bitch, fight, fight!" yelled Veronica.

"I will, you fucking ugly freak, I'll fuck you up," shouted Shakira.

They went back and forth for what seemed like the rest of the day. I didn't see how they thought they could ever get the chance to fight with a room of twenty Staff holding them down to the ground. They couldn't even blow their noses, let alone punch someone else. But they didn't calm down or even let up for over an hour. Shakira got tranquilized, but Veronica went on taunting Staff and singing her nursery rhymes between swears.

The fights between Veronica and Shakira continued for two days. There's nothing more pathetic than hearing two morons thinking they can fight each other when being held down by twenty Staff. During that time I was able to figure out how the restraining system worked. The Staff on STU, and the other night Staff, always had these strange necklaces around their necks. At the end of the necklace there were big blue buttons, just like the ones old paranoid people wear in case they fall down and can't get up. The Staff would push the buttons whenever they were in trouble, and it would send off the alarm. Other Staff would hear it and seemed to run out of the middle of nowhere to come and help.

Staff started to feel sorry for us, having to listen to the trash talking and alarms all the time. So they gave us ice cream and let us watch movies. Pretty nice reward for watching other kids lose it.

Then, later that night, I saw Staff run. But this time they went to the Trusted Area. I heard Amy yell and Rochelle scream as they were escorted out of the room and put in different corners of the Day Room.

"I swear we said nothing," Rochelle whined.

"We heard you. Don't lie, Rochelle!"

They moved Rochelle's and Amy's mattresses to different sides of the Day Room.

TIME: 7:38 pm   **PATIENT NAME: Abigail Vona**

Group Treatment note: Patient told the group that she "daydreams" and has trouble focusing. Abigail stated, " I think about movies and stories, I make things up in my head."

- Dr. K. Wisely

Chapter -2

SHADOW PUPPET

Day 59

The next day, during Group, Miss Curran spoke first. "Last night you might have heard Amy and Rochelle interacting in the Trusted Area."

I scanned the Group and focused on Rochelle. I felt sorry for her. When I looked at Amy rocking back and forth, I was glad they caught her for being sneaky.

"Amy," Miss Blankered's southern accent turned cold and intimidating. "Tell us what happened last night."

"Nothing, I promise. We were doing nothing."

I was angry that she didn't tell the truth, and I was angry that she lied so well. Was that what she did at home? Give her parents the perfect act and destroy her sister's life? Is that what she was trying to do with Rochelle?

"So Rochelle, tell us what happened?" asked Miss Blankered, giving up on a straight answer from Amy.

Rochelle choked and started to cry. Unlike Amy, she wasn't a liar.

Rochelle's attitude had changed dramatically and she was doing a whole lot better on STU. Her ghetto-fab manner had changed. She had become a happy young girl, laughing at silly things and cracking corny jokes with Staff. I wondered whether, if Shakira ever got out of bed, then Rochelle would go back to the tough-girl act. If I had just met Rochelle, I would never have believed that she'd had sex, let alone been a prostitute.

Rochelle explained, her voice stopping and starting, "Well, at first, we said, 'hello' and 'thanks' whenever we passed our meals, when nobody else was around." Amy's expression turned to pure hatred at Rochelle's unexpected confession. Now Rochelle was out of Amy's control.

"Then last night, we whispered about movies and our favorite colors. It was fun." Amy rocked faster, gnawing on her fingernails.

Miss Curran stared at them. "Both of you will permanently be moved from the Trusted Area." she said firmly. "Abby and Katherine will move into your places."

Miss Curran gave me and Katherine a smile. I felt like I could fly! *They trust me*. Two months ago, they didn't trust me with plastic spoons. Katherine was so happy too, she was like that more now. It was like she had been brought back to life these past couple of weeks.

"Perhaps some of you noticed," preached Miss Blankered, "but last night, Amy finally showed her true nature."

Everyone seemed shocked to hear this except Rochelle, Amy, and me. "Well, last night," Miss Blankered continued, "Rochelle interacted for kicks, but Amy was angry. She simply wanted to get back at us for not giving her a Focus. You see, Amy will never tell you this, but I'm going to say it for her . . ."

Amy rocked faster and faster, until I waited for her to spin off the floor.

"Amy is afraid. She tests people. She does things both for control and to see your reaction. She has absolutely no trust in the world nor anybody in it. She thinks everyone is either like her parents or her adopted parents and she will go to any lengths just to get a reaction from you. This is how she protects herself."

Amy looked up and stared evilly at the Group.

"You see," continued Miss Blankered, "Amy's parents abused and neglected her. Amy and her brother and sister were found starving before they landed in state custody. They were quickly adopted by a couple. Unfortunately, the mother was overprotective. Your Focus, Amy, is: what is the difference between how you act here, and how you act at home? The answer is: there is no difference. You're just as scared, just as fake, just as controlling. It's just harder for you to do it here than at home, where you can prey upon your eight-year-old sister and ten-year-old brother. At home, there aren't twenty Staff watching you every minute of the day."

Amy was biting her nails to the point I thought she was going to tear them right off.

"Group over," snapped Miss Blankered.

TIME: 11:37 pm   **PATIENT NAME: Abigail Vona**

Milieu Treatment note: Patient was escorted to Time Out at 7:35 pm—7:45 pm for biting on her fingers (self-injurious behaviors) despite being told not to do this. Patient was able to tell staff she was angry at them for prompting behavior. Patient seemed tearful.

- R. Curran

Day 60

I got another letter from my mom. This time it had a sticky note from Miss Fawn saying, "Process this in Group!"

Dear Abby,
I am at home now and thinking of you. I really miss you so much and wish I could be in Family Therapy with you. I think this would help

us improve our relationship and also help you grow and heal. I hope you understand that people aren't always what they seem to be. Your dad presents himself as a kind man, going through the course of life and being a successful doctor. But in all sincerity, he is only selfish, caring about his own needs. I know now that I shouldn't have married him, and that I made a mistake before you were even born. All I want is for you to understand what kind of a man your "nice" father really is.

When Elizabeth was eleven or twelve, your dad and I took her down to the Florida caves. They were big, dark and difficult to find our way around, but it felt like a fun adventure. Well, Elizabeth panicked and started to get scared and cry. What does your father do? Of course he decides that he is suddenly claustrophobic and pushes us out of the way, running off. To this day, he'll never admit it because he is dishonest and uncaring. He is doing the same thing with your Family Therapist. He's bribing her to let him be the only one having Therapy with you. He wants to make sure that we can't speak. I know that all he wants to do is hurt me.

The letter went on and on about how my dad is two-faced. It was one of many "Your Dad's a Fuck" stories that I had gotten used to. But when I read it this time, my instinct was to ask myself whether she was really telling the truth.

My mom and dad hated each other and they had felt like that towards each other before I was even born. They hated to agree on things. It made it practically impossible for either one to punish me because each contradicted the other's authority, which worked great for me. The down side was that I never knew who or what to believe — my mom exaggerated and my dad was in denial of everything.

I don't even know why my sister is the way she is because they gave me two entirely different stories. My mom told me repeatedly that it was my dad's fault because the nurse at the hospital wasn't qualified and fucked up the pregnancy, causing my sister to have a stroke and be born with autism. Then she said my dad beat her for misbehaving and when my sister got her period the next day, that's when she had her schizophrenic breakdown. Of course my dad said my sister was born fucked up and it didn't help that my mom's brother, who was a drug dealer at the time, gave her a pot brownie at the age of three.

I just knew I didn't want to end up like my older sister.

TIME: 9:42 pm   **PATIENT NAME: Abigail Vona**

Group Treatment note: Patient processed a letter from her mother this session. Patient seemed to have a hard time realizing what was inappropriate in it. Patient stated "I don't see my mother as a mother. I see her as my sister."

- Dr. K. Wisely

Day 61

At Group Therapy, Dr. Wisely called on Rochelle first.

"I'll talk about last night's interacting and also about the second time I got raped."

"Okay Rochelle," Dr. Wisely interrupted, "But why do you choose to do that?"

"Because, I want to get both off my chest."

Rochelle looked at Dr. Wisely, searching for approval, and he nodded it was fine to go on.

"Last night, I was such an idiot. I lost trust." Tears started down her face. "I have Family Therapy tomorrow . . . I mean, what the hell am I going to tell my mom? She was so proud of how I was doing!"

I felt really bad for Rochelle; she seemed to be doing everything here to prove herself. To everyone, but to her own family most of all. She honestly cared about them, probably even more than she cared about herself.

"I remember my second rape. Joaquin, my partner . . . my pimp, had me working real hard." She had stopped crying, she was fine now. Her mention of a pimp gave me a much clearer picture of how serious a prostitute she actually was. *How many men has she been with?*

"This guy, like, picked me up and offered me fifty dollars. I said, yeah, but only for thirty minutes. Well, he spent the first fifteen minutes driving out of town. He said it was because he didn't want anyone he knew to see him. I didn't think anything of it. So we went to an empty road in a nature preserve. He was real rough, and I told him to chill the fuck out, but it got real bad when he took out his knife. That's when I knew I was in some serious shit. I managed to get the hell out of there and he chased me through the woods until I screamed and screamed and finally some family who were camping nearby came over. I think he got scared so he ran. I was all cut up and embarrassed . . . I never saw him again."

She told her story like Dr. Wisely described, as though it was only gossip. She could talk about getting raped and nearly murdered like it wasn't such a big deal. It was almost like it wasn't Rochelle speaking. When she finished, she called on Amy.

Amy didn't remove her hands from her mouth, making the words hard to hear. "I call time to talk about what happened last night." Her words were monotone and drained — a drastic change from her peppy, jumpy self.

"Everything Dr. Wisely said is true. I do kind of test you, like the way I test my brother and sister."

She admitted it, and seemed like she couldn't care less. The

Group looked stunned. I wasn't. Amy waited for one of us to say something, but no one did.

"Amy," said Dr. Wisely, "this is one major step for you, and you just earned your Focus."

Amy just sat there stiffly.

"We cannot help you here anymore, so time to make big steps and some real connections. Welcome to the Frog Clan."

Amy went whiter than white, then froze like a star on a Christmas tree, no rocking.

I couldn't believe Amy was actually going, I thought she would be here forever. For some weird reason, I didn't want her to go. *I want it to be me. I so want it to be me.*

Then Veronica avoided her Focus and talked about how much she wanted a sex change.

Amy left that afternoon after Group.

Late that afternoon, while I timed Rochelle into the bathroom, Katherine's hand went up and Miss Curran called on her. "Safety or medical?" I stepped over to look but suddenly tripped, getting a nasty rope burn from the rug.

"Medical *and* safety," said Katherine.

"What is it?" asked Miss Curran.

"Can I tell you in private?" asked Katherine, rushing up to Miss Curran with a long metal wire in her hand.

The wire looked like it belonged to the braces on her teeth. *Did Katherine take off the wires from her braces? To cut herself?* Katherine rolled up her sleeves and all I could see were her sliced arms. I couldn't believe it. I thought Katherine was over it. She had changed so much, I didn't understand. All I knew was the moment Katherine showed Miss Curran her cuts, they moved her straight back to her old bed, leaving Rochelle to move back to the Trusted Area with me.

It wasn't until seven o'clock when things finally calmed down that I was able to show Staff my rope burn from landing on the rug. I usually didn't care much about cuts and burns, but with Staff, everything was suspect. Even a tiny cut mattered, because for all they knew, I could have been mutilating myself. I took extra care not to have them suspect me of doing any of that, especially after being on Suicide Precautions, which was the second worst experience of my life.

I raised my hand to Miss Curran.

"Yes, Abby, safety or medical?"

"Medical, I've got a rope burn." I went over and showed her my arm. It was flaming red and parts of it were scabbed right over. I spent the next few minutes cleaning it. Miss Curran got ice for me and put it on.

"See, Abby, when you feel something cold, your mind focuses on the cold instead of the pain," said Miss Curran, pressing an ice pack over my skin.

I thought about how ice helped cut pain, but cold still fucking hurt, too. I had never thought about it that way before — the one pain helped get rid of the other pain, but they both still hurt.

TIME: 3:35 pm **PATIENT NAME: Abigail Vona**

Milieu Treatment note: Patient seemed to enjoy her birthday party yet seemed somewhat awkward and overwhelmed. Patient seemed compliant.

— R. Curran

Day 62

Katherine sat with her sleeves rolled up, embarrassed.

"Is the Group okay with Katherine starting off?" ordered

Miss Curran. Katherine sighed like a drama queen. "I call time, to tell you all why I cut on myself . . . I was upset because Amy left, that's all." She started to cry.

"Is that really why you did it, Katherine?" asked Miss Curran. "I think you did it for attention. When you cut on yourself before, you hid it. Now you flaunt it. You told us seconds after you did it."

Katherine stared at Miss Curran with her big pug-dog eyes and a dumbstruck expression. She looked more like a China doll now than ever before. "I . . . I . . . I did it all because, before you paid attention to me, and now you don't," she whimpered.

There was an awkward silence before Rochelle broke it, "Next time, if you want attention, Katherine, tell us!"

No one asks for attention, they do things for attention. They become prostitutes, bulimics, drug addicts. Every problem stems from wanting attention. In a perfect world, we would probably just ask for attention. But it doesn't work that way.

Katherine livened up at the idea of simply asking for attention though she knew we weren't allowed to talk.

TIME: 8:45 pm   **PATIENT NAME: Abigail Vona**

Group Treatment note: Patient expressed, "During the party I was feeling really happy at times. I felt something I'm not used to. I felt safe and cared about. When I just came in the room, it was like a dream. I got this warm feeling inside, but my face looks sad. I've had that feeling before, but not much. When a boy at summer camp once gave me a bracelet, when my dad once said goodnight when he thought I was asleep." Patient then appeared to abruptly change subject.

- Dr. K. Wisely

Day 77

The Trusted Area improved my life. I appreciated not having Staff watch my every move and I got to do things freely that I couldn't normally do. For one, I could make shadow puppets in the rays of light through the window.

I spent early Sunday watching the Groups out in the Cabins and thinking of how much I envied them. They actually let Shakira go back to the Coyotes, which was hard to believe. I saw Mary power-walking up a hill, red-faced. They were out in the sun. It was almost September. I had been here for almost three months and I did the same thing every day. But somehow, I had changed in this one room these past few weeks. Rochelle and Katherine had, too.

The next day was when we got our Focuses. I had the feeling that at least one of us, Rochelle, Katherine, or I, would end up going to the Cabins. I hoped it would be me, but I was afraid at the same time.

All three of us had grown up so much. Rochelle had gone from ghetto tough to playful girl. If she went home now, would she go back to her pimp?

The first time I saw Katherine she seemed like she spent her life at a funeral. Now she hopped around like a hyperactive puppy. But she would go back to cutting on herself if she didn't get attention or if people made fun of her.

And me. I came here without a care or responsibility in the world, and now I ran the whole unit. I knew that if I went home tomorrow, or in a week, or in a month, or even in a year, I would go back to Matt, go back to my old friends, do the same things and not look back, never look back. I might feel bad for a while, but I would get over it. Maybe I would get a job, but I'd still do the same things.

I thought about my friends. School had started this week. *I wonder if they're thinking of me. I would die to talk to one of my friends. I miss them so much. But out of everybody, I especially miss Matt.*

That night I sat on my bed and thought about him. I felt like a ho for cheating on him with Keno. But then I thought of the true ho, Rochelle. That made me feel better. I wasn't bad at all, really. I wondered how Rochelle could fuck so many guys and be able to live with it, or if she really was just a prostitute at heart. I was not a bad girl, I was just doing teenage stuff — Rochelle was the fucked up one here.

TIME: 2:15 pm **PATIENT NAME: Abigail Vona**

Group Treatment note: Patient stated "I've been thinking of my family a lot. I feel more supported here than at home."

- Dr. K. Wisely

Day 86

We circled up for Group. Dr. Wisely pulled out his papers. "Veronica, there is no one to impress. We would like to get to know who you really are. Katherine, you made leaps and bounds in your treatment, don't fall back to old behaviors and sabotage yourself. Abby, you're ready to move on, but you need to learn the world doesn't always revolve around you. We are proud of your accomplishments. Now it's time for you to learn patience."

My Focus not only confused me, it also made me mad.

"Rochelle, welcome to the Coyote Clan where you will find yourself!"

Katherine and I grinded our teeth in jealousy, even though we were happy for Rochelle.

When Rochelle left that afternoon, I missed her the moment she walked out the door, smiling and crying into the sun. I thought at that moment I would never see her again. Funny, I never really thought of Rochelle as a friend because they never really allowed us to make friends. We hardly ever spoke. But now when I considered it, we were real friends.

TIME: 6:31 pm   **PATIENT NAME: Abigail Vona**

Individual Psychotherapy note: Abigail described how a recent departure of a peer affected her. She described feeling quite saddened and distracted as a result of missing the departed peer. She reflected on their relationship as a means to explore why the departure had such an effect.

- Dr. K. Wisely

Day 87

Katherine and I had a feeling we would be off next. Both our Focuses said it. I thought about my Focus and it made sense now. *You're ready, but the world doesn't revolve around you* meant I was ready, but the Cabins were probably full. I had one lesson to learn on STU. And that was patience. My Group, as fucked up as they were, helped me out, and Staff, as much as I hated them, did the same thing.

Later that day, I had Family Therapy. To my surprise, my dad was really encouraging. He told me to be strong and good, and that before I knew it, I'd be out. And for some reason, I felt better than I'd ever felt since before I left home.

Day 105

TIME: 5:23 pm   **PATIENT NAME:** Abigail Vona

Group Treatment note: Patient expressed feeling "nervous, scared, and sad." Patient stated, "I feel like I'm in my own little world. I'm nervous about tomorrow. I don't miss things until I don't have it. I don't know how to say goodbye. I am scared and I am trying to look at it positively. When I leave it is going to hit me hard. I think I'm going to have to prepare myself. I don't know how to prepare myself. I'm scared." Patient seemed genuine about her feelings. Patient offered nothing further.

- Dr. K. Wisely

Chapter -1

TWERKS, CAPS, AND SNIPPER

Day 106

The September air felt cool, a lot different than June air, the last time I was outside. The sun was piercing and my eyes took a moment to adjust. I was finally in real clothes. Well, sort of. Early in the morning, Miss Curran had walked onto the unit with a pile of new clothes and said, "Your dad gave us money to go to Target and get some clothes for the Cabins. All your things were either too small, or just not warm enough." They were ugly, didn't go together, and were three sizes bigger than what I used to wear. But that wasn't really the problem. The problem was that right now my stomach felt like it was full of cockroaches.

The day before when Dr. Wisely called my name, I felt my heart stop. "Abby, welcome to the Coyote Clan, where you'll become a true leader in your own life."

I didn't know what to think, or what to feel. It was like someone had just ripped out the whole of my insides, scraping until there was nothing left, nothing to think or feel. I felt blackness. The idea of the change is what scared me so much.

Now I stared at the change. Trees outlined a road and there was a tall totem pole that had decayed so much you couldn't make out the animal faces carved into it. Next to the rotting pole was a trail with two women walking toward me. One was tall with short blond hair. The other dark-haired woman I had seen once before, on STU, during Shakira's restraint: the cool cowboy woman. She still had a chubby face and brown squirrel-eyes, but no pigtails. She had chopped her hair into a bob.

"Hi, I'm Miss Strickler." She looked straight at me. She knew who I was. "I'm the Staff member in charge of the Coyote Clan. I'm here to pick you up, Abby."

I looked over at Katherine, who was with the blond woman. Katherine was looking at me. I didn't know if we were allowed to speak so I just looked in her direction and nodded "goodbye." Even that was more contact than we were allowed.

Miss Strickler grabbed my bags and told me to follow her. She led me onto a trail into the forest. It was just the two of us. And the only thing I could think about was running. I would not run, not yet.

I had so many questions, but I didn't know if I could speak. Did I have to raise my hand? Here in the forest?

"So Abby, you excited about the Cabins?" asked Miss Strickler, splintering the silence. "Or don't you speak?" She gave a slight chuckle.

"Oh," I said, grateful to hear my own voice outside, "I didn't know."

"Well, the Cabins are different than STU, takes a while to get used to the rules."

I wasn't sure if different was a really good thing or a really bad thing. I had kind of just gotten used to the rules on STU.

"When we get to the Cabins, you'll be paired up with a 'three-foot-buddy,' who will explain all the rules to you. The first week, you're on 'grace.' That means, we're gracious enough not to give you any Consequences. But I strongly recommend you do some push-ups with the Group. Work your muscles."

"Is that the punishment we get, push-ups?"

"First of all these are *Consequences*, right? Punishments imply that we are just downright mean. Consequences derive from your bad behavior."

Her hard eyes could have shattered steel.

"And second of all, don't interrupt me, or you'll get a Consequence — grace or not. You still need to learn that it was only you and your behavior that put you in a level-three lockdown, nobody else."

I wanted to yell out, "My sicko stepmom and abusive dad put me in here!" But I knew she would probably just send me back to STU and have one of the other girls take my place in the Cabins. So I just shut my mouth and walked the trail.

It wasn't long before we came out of the woods and into a clearing. We walked straight towards a square log cabin, which looked abandoned.

Miss Strickler rummaged around in her pocket for a set of keys. I turned around to have a look at my surroundings. Everywhere I looked I saw mountains, trees, and squirrels. It wasn't much different than Connecticut. Miss Strickler opened the door. It was dark inside, and there was no furniture except for seven bunk beds and a desk. In the middle of the room was an old-fashioned stove which burned wood, making the air dry like in a sauna. The cabin was rustic inside and out. It had six windows, but they weren't barred. Everything was made of wood and it was small. The only modern thing in the whole room was a single light bulb that hung from the ceiling. I looked around the cabin for a door that led to a bathroom but couldn't find one. Next to the stove were five girls and Dr. Wisely, sitting together, in a circle.

Of the five girls, I knew four of them: Dannie, Mary, Rochelle, and Shakira. The whole Group turned to look at me. They all had goofy smiles. A woman sat in one of the only chairs in the cabin taking notes. I was glad to see Dr. Wisely.

Dannie's hand shot up in the air. Miss Strickler nodded. "Excuse me, Miss Strickler and Miss Rossly, can the Group say 'Hi' to Abby and may Shakira be her three-foot-buddy?" Dannie looked so different. Her skin was tanned and her eyes had brightened. All the girls looked healthier from how I remembered them on STU.

"Yes and no," said Miss Strickler, "Do you think it's appropriate that Shakira have the privilege of three-foot when she only came back here a few days ago? Am I wrong?"

The Group said, "No, ma'am," in unison, except for the girl I didn't know, who seemed preoccupied with a leaf, instead of what Miss Strickler was saying. Dannie raised her hand again.

"Yes Dannie, what is it?"

"May Mary go on three-foot with Abby?" Dannie didn't look as confident now.

Miss Strickler stood there for a moment before answering, "Yup, Abby, go on over with Mary, your new three-foot-buddy."

I walked over to the circle and sat between Mary and Dannie. They smiled at me, and Mary handed me a rope. "It's a three-foot rope," Mary said. "See, here in the Cabins, your three-foot buddy tells you the rules, so you need to stay close. The rope makes sure that you and I are together. It's not a punishment. It's a precaution."

I knew the rules were different around here, but I was freaked out that Mary had spoken to me without asking first. I didn't like it. Who knows what they might say if they could talk all the time?

Mary then gave me one end of the old rope and picked up the other end so we were joined together. Even though Mary had assured me it wasn't a punishment, I felt punished. Actually, I felt like a dog on a leash.

I didn't have time to ponder my situation before Mary started explaining, "We're in Group Therapy and since you're here, we are going to have an introduction Group, like on STU."

Dr. Wisely nodded to Shakira.

"Hello . . ." Shakira yawned. "I'm Shakira. I've been here more than once. This time, I've been here for thirteen months." She had a look of venom, when reminded how long her stay had been.

She cracked her knuckles. "Next," she said, mocking how Dr. Wisely spoke.

The girl I didn't know laughed, and Miss Strickler turned to look at both girls.

"That's not funny, Candace and Shakira."

Shakira gave Miss Strickler one of her fierce looks.

"You know better, Shakira," Miss Strickler scolded, not giving into Shakira's intimidation.

"I expect a page of apology to Dr. Wisely. You just came off 'Shut Down'. It would be a shame." I looked over at Dr. Wisely, who didn't seem to mind Shakira's humor. "Go ahead, Dannie."

"Hi, I'm Dannie. I'm here for abusing my parents. I've been here for four months. I'm working on expressing my anger, and I'm the Group Leader, that means I sort of run things, like you did on STU. Only out here it's a privilege and that's about it. Mary?"

I presumed Dannie was still a dyke.

"Hi, I'm Mary. I've been here for two months. I got put here for abuse of cocaine, and weed, and having sex with many partners."

This was a surprise. On STU, Saint Mary didn't do drugs or anything and now all this. I thought she was like me. I had no idea that she was the biggest liar, slut, and druggie in the world. What made her crack?

"I'm working on expressing my compulsions to smoke and do drugs. Also, I'm focusing on being more real to myself and others. That's about it. Rochelle?"

I wondered what else Mary wasn't telling.

Rochelle had definitely gotten over looking up to Shakira.

"Hi, I'm Rochelle," she said blowing her nose before going on. "I've been here three and a half months. I got put here for doing different drugs, mostly cocaine, for being a prostitute, for stealing, lying, running away, and basically acting wild. Candace?"

Candace was still transfixed by the limp leaf she had in her hand. She looked sort of pretty when you first glanced at her but then you noticed how flawed she was. Her eyes were a pretty color, but shaped funny. Her nose was perfect but didn't fit right on her face. Her mouth was crooked. It was weird, like she was supposed to be gorgeous, but something went wrong. Before speaking, she slowly put the leaf down and looked around the room, as though she had just woken up.

"Hi, my name is Candace." She had a look that was out of it.

"I was put in here . . . 'cause I worship the devil." She paused to look me straight in the eyes. "I took lots of drugs and used to steal from stores." She twirled the leaf in her hand and looked at it.

I didn't really know what to think of Candace. The whole room waited for her to continue but she just played with the leaf.

Miss Strickler spoke up, "Stop acting gamey. Put the leaf down and explain why you're here."

Candace came back to life but still acted defiant. "I was put here for using cocaine, angel dust, crack, heroin, weed, crystal meth, steroids, dope, Ritalin, amphetamines, pain killers, uppers, downers, twerks, caps, alcohol, and snipper."

Twerks, caps, snipper?

"I was also here before. And, I am a cutter, bulimic, anorexic, a pyromaniac, and I like to fuck . . . a lot. I'm working on being open and honest."

"Now, Abby," Mary said, "you get to talk."

I nodded my head, letting Mary know I understood the drill. "Well, I got put here for running away . . ."

I decided to tell more just so that I would have something to work on so that I could get out of here. Besides, I wanted them to think I was a bad girl too. ". . . and for smoking weed and drinking alcohol three times." Now, the truth is I hated alcohol, and weed didn't satisfy me. I just did it to fit in, the same reason I was talking about it here. I thought about more stuff I did. I had stolen money from my dad and used to steal from stores too.

"And stealing." I looked around. They all just sat there. I decided it was safe to go on. "I've been here for three months, and that's about it."

Mary asked, "How do you feel about coming out to the Cabins?"

I hated answering questions like that. It was obvious how I felt. I was scared. Who wouldn't be? I was scared of going back to STU, scared of living here, and scared I would never go home.

"I'm feeling all right." I didn't want to tell them the truth.

"I would like to express," said Candace. She looked at the ceiling as if something fascinating was up there, then she slowly brought her eyes down as if she was touched by something from above, like a wacko holy man would. "I still love Satan, I do . . . I really do."

I looked at the others girls' faces. Shakira rolled her eye with a "here we go again" expression. Dannie looked like she wanted to break Candace's neck and everyone else looked, well, nervous.

"I want Marilyn. I thought of him again last night." She must have been talking about Marilyn Manson. If you're going to be a freak, be a creative one — Marilyn Manson is what every boring-ass kid who wants to frighten their parents, and the principal at school, says they like.

"Candace, why are you saying this?" Dr. Wisely asked, in a bored tone like there was no hope he could bring this girl back to sanity.

"I want to be honest," Candace said sweetly.

Dannie thundered, "Time to take a porta!"

"We have to line up at the door and get into formation," Mary told me.

I looked at the Group and noticed they were in two straight lines. I remembered the Groups doing this when I saw them from the window STU. "Sometimes, like today, as a Consequence we all have to carry a long rope to keep us in better formation. We always have to walk from place to place in a straight line."

Candace and Shakira came over with an orange water container. It looked very heavy. Candace panted from carrying it, and Shakira bitched about Candace not picking up enough of the container.

"That's the Gott," Mary said, with a laugh. "It's very heavy. We have to carry it wherever we go, in case of emergencies, and we use it for drinking water. It's full of ice and water; the good news is it gets lighter as the day goes on."

The perfect line thing reminded me of the Madeline children's books, only this was not fun.

Across from the cabin, there were three portable toilets, like the ones you get at concerts and campsites. I avoided going into portable toilets. I'd gag every time I went into one. They are fucking gross.

It took a while for us to reach them, because Candace, acting like she was hurt, dropped her side of the Gott, leaving Shakira swearing in utter frustration. If Candace wasn't a Satan-worshipping, hypochondriac, nut-case, I would have felt sorry for her. It was only ten yards to the portas, but that ten yards took ten minutes.

When we got there, we had a total of five minutes for all of us to use the three "portas."

Dannie counted down the minutes out loud.

I must have been blue from lack of oxygen when I came out and got back into line.

Five minutes later, Dannie was shouting, "We are going over time!" When we finished, she raised her hand.

"Excuse me, Miss Strickler and Miss Rossly. May I make you aware, we went two minutes over our time goal. May we please have Consequences?"

Dannie said this like it was an everyday routine.

Miss Strickler sighed and asked Miss Rossly what she thought.

"Two pyramid tens," said Miss Rossly, who was red-headed and very pretty.

As soon as she said this, the entire Group moaned and dropped to the ground.

"You don't have to do this. You're on grace," Mary said to me.

I decided not to join in, and was glad I didn't. The exercise was confusing — they did two push-ups, then two sit-ups, then three, then four, all the way up to ten. Then they went back down again all the way to one. Mary later told me that each pyramid was a hundred push-ups and sit-ups. No wonder everyone looked healthier.

Once they finished, we got back into formation and walked. I heard Miss Rossly say, "Be respectful."

As soon as she said that, every girl in the Group put her head down, looking at the ground as if hypnotized. I, on the other hand, didn't know what they were doing and looked around. All I saw was a trail in the woods, which opened up to a clearing and a big stone building. But then I heard footsteps behind me and turned. There was a group of about eight boys in their own formation, passing us. They too had their heads down. This was the first time I had seen boys up close in months. I would have done anything just to talk to them or hang out. Something told me I would like southern guys. Suddenly, I realized the rule. I quickly put my head down, but it was too late.

Miss Strickler pounced on me, "Abby!" she shouted, "Your whole Group puts their heads down, and you look up to see what's going on. Are you that oblivious to your surroundings?"

I didn't like being lectured, and she had a way of making me feel like a child. Her gaze soon left me and focused on Mary who looked terrified.

"Mary!" Miss Strickler went on. "You're obviously not doing your job. Your three-foot buddy doesn't know the rules. You're not explaining anything to her!"

Then there was an uncomfortable silence, as Miss Strickler stared at the Group. "And the rest of you all, where were you?"

They just stood there, still in formation, Candace and Shakira holding the Gott.

"Well, since you're not doing what you're supposed to do and not taking care of your new Group member, I think you need to do another pyramid ten. Now!" The Group groaned and dropped to the ground for the Consequence. I didn't want to join in and wouldn't have if Miss Strickler didn't glare at me and point to the dirt. I dropped to the ground and joined in.

One push-up, one sit-up, two push-ups, two sit-ups . . . it was hurting on the second one. Going up to ten? My body had been sitting on a bed for three months. I was at nine, going down, and I gave up. I couldn't do anymore. I just sat there as the Group of girls went on with their exercise. I knew that when I got off this grace thing I would hate it. I felt guilty that I got the Group into trouble, but mostly I was furious with Miss Strickler. I hadn't meant to look. Even Miss Blankered wasn't such a bitch.

We got to the building, which had an identical door and windows on each side. It was split in half by a brick wall, so you couldn't see at the other side.

"This is the cafeteria," Mary explained. "This is the girls' side and the other side is the boys'."

I looked over at the boys' side, and Mary practically shouted to stop me, "No! You can't look over there!" It wasn't like her to flip out.

"One of the most important rules of the Cabins is respecting other clans. We stay away from the boys' clans as much as possible."

What was the big deal? It wasn't like I never saw boys before. *And when I get out of this place I'm pretty sure I'll do more than just look at them.*

"Every time we look at a boy and get caught by a peer, we have to do a pyramid ten. Every time we get caught by Staff, then the whole Group gets in trouble."

We walked into the cafeteria. My spirits improved — I saw desserts and a salad bar. I hadn't had dessert for three months. That was a record for me. When I was out in the real world, if I was on a diet, skipping dessert was an accomplishment. Being here, I wasn't trying to impress anyone with being thin and sexy, so this was great.

I watched Miss Strickler make her way to the tray of cookies. She started eating them in front of all of us. They looked so good. She didn't exactly need any cookies, though. She could have used a diet.

We had to wait in line while Shakira, Rochelle, and Candace set up plates, silverware, and napkins. The walls were painted bright yellow, reminding me of a kindergarten classroom. I wondered if they chose the color thinking that it would have a therapeutic effect. The ceiling of the cafeteria was high, and brightly colored banners hung from the top. There were pictures of animals and poems. I saw one that said Frog Clan, but none said Coyote. Others said Swan Clan, Cougar Clan, and even Spider Clan. I wondered when or if these other clans still existed.

We all circled around the table, and Miss Strickler ordered us to say a silent prayer. Even though praying was never a priority for me, I thought it was a little strange that we prayed before the food was in front of us. I guess they made that rule because I couldn't see Candace or Shakira praying seriously when there was a plate of food in front of them.

We went up to get food in a line. I had so missed choosing my own food.

The food bar faced the kitchen, and I got a good look at the cooks. Like every other cafeteria, the cooks were some of the nastiest people I ever saw. My only problem about eating cafeteria food was the people who prepared it. A fear of mine consisted of kitchen help doing crazy, disgusting things like dunking fries in toilets and spitting on eggs. I had made it a habit to always be nice to whoever served my food for this exact reason.

Once we all got our food we went back to our tables in pairs. As soon as we got back to our table Mary scolded me, "Abby, you don't have a vegetable, and you took way too many fries. We can't have any desserts when you don't eat with proper nutrition."

I looked at the cookies in my hand and wanted to eat them so much, but Mary took them from me. She led me to the trash where she threw them away. Then she threw hers away, too.

"It was my fault," she said, frowning, "I should have been a better three-foot buddy." She then led me back to the food bar to fill up on the nastiest vegetable things I ever saw. The way she punished herself, too, shocked and impressed me. I would have to be like that someday if I wanted to get out of here. I wondered if the greenish weed-like food was a southern thing, or the cook's toilet special.

During the mealtime, we were allowed to talk about "superficial" things with each other. These consisted of movies that were less than PG-13, pets, the weather, sports, and things like that. The pill woman walked in and called us up individually to take our pills. I wasn't used to talking and felt uneasy when Dannie asked me what I liked to do for fun. I wanted to say "Everything that got me sent here!" but I didn't think Miss Strickler, who was listening to our conversation, would appreciate that comment. I was relieved when the pill woman called me. I searched my mind for something "fun" that wouldn't get me into trouble while she handed me my pill. I looked at my palm — I only got one pill now, the little green Paxil.

I went back to the table and told Dannie, "Well . . . I like movies." The girls all talked like they were on a sixth grade playground, speaking in baby ghetto words that were out of date like "girlfriend" this and that and "No, you didn't." I didn't know how to relate and couldn't believe that a bunch of ex-prostitutes and drug addicts were sitting at a table doing knock-knock jokes and reminiscing about their favorite scenes from *The Little* fucking *Mermaid*.

Dannie giggled. "What movies are your favorites?" She acted like she was five. Again, I searched my mind for a movie that wasn't rated R. This girl acted like a child, so I said *Babe*. I couldn't picture Dannie doing drugs, getting restrained, or swearing even. But I knew from my time on STU that all these girls were capable of doing that and much more. I talked to Dannie the whole meal. Talking was nice.

As we got ready to leave, Shakira's hand shot up. "Excuse me, Miss Strickler and Miss Rossly, can I call a Confront Group?"

We stood around in a circle. My stomach had a sort of drum roll when I heard "Confront."

"Excuse me, Candace," Shakira said with a look of triumph on her face. "I'm Confronting you for dropping a spoon and then setting it, instead of getting a clean one."

Candace rolled her eyes at Shakira. "All right," she said, like she didn't care. "Group," said Candace, "May I have a Consequence?"

Even though Candace wasn't taking this seriously she sounded so admirable.

Shakira was the first to speak, and something told me she enjoyed provoking Candace.

"I suggest meal separation," she said, holding back a smirk.

"I suggest a pyramid ten," Rochelle said.

"I suggest twenty push-ups," Mary said. I think Mary felt some tension and wanted to calm Candace down.

Miss Strickler must have picked up on this too. "Mary, Mary, Mary," she said sternly, "If you can't face other people's problems, how on earth are you going to face your own?"

Mary took Miss Strickler's words hard and stared at the ground, a look of humiliation engraved on her face.

With three suggestions, the Group then voted on the pyramid ten, and we waited while Candace did it.

The day went on, and my head hurt with all the new things I had to learn. Mary constantly told me more and more, but like a wet sponge my brain couldn't absorb anymore.

Then we had to walk a full mile away from the cabin to the bathhouse. The place had twelve showers and a place for us to do laundry once a week. It looked shabby — the paint was chipping and some of the tiles on the floor were flaking off. We had to shower and then clean up everything before leaving. Staff would insure this by inspecting the bathhouse after we were done. For every hair that was found, we had to do a push-up. Miss Strickler had a sharp eye and usually found at least fifty hairs.

When we finally got back to the Cabins, it was almost time for bed. We had fifteen minutes to write a letter home. I didn't bother.

TIME: 3:12 pm   **PATIENT NAME: Abigail Vona**

Group Treatment note: Patient stated "I'm feeling very overwhelmed . . . I didn't have a good day in the Cabins, I feel nervous out there. I felt like coming back to STU."

- Dr. K. Wisely

Chapter 1

COMPULSION

Day 107

I was still awake after midnight. My first night in the cabin seemed to last forever. I woke up seven times from Rochelle's snoring. And I had trouble getting used to sleeping in the dark, in contrast to the bright lights of STU. I thought about running away all night since Staff seemed to be sound asleep. But then I remembered there were bells on the doors that jingled whenever you opened them. Plus the Staff beds were right next to the door.

When the sun started to come up above the mountains, an alarm went off and someone yelled, "Coyotes, get up!"

"Time to make our beds," Dannie shouted. I was lost as everyone did stuff. Miss Strickler sat on her bed looking comfortable with her extra pink pillows and giving Candace Consequences for being rude.

Mary, my three-foot buddy, told me all about what an exciting day of "Twelve Step Reflection" we were going to have. But she forgot to tell me simple things I needed to know, like where to put my pajamas. And she didn't tell me the rule about tucking your shirt in, so I got yelled at by Miss Strickler. It was a while before we got to the portas. I dreaded the portas, but had no choice but to use them. When it was my turn, I opened the door to the familiar smells of chemicals and feces, which had me instantly grabbing my nose and almost suffocating.

The whole day was supposed to be spent in the cabin working on our addictions, whatever that meant. Rochelle and Dannie went to the bookshelf and pulled down identical big blue books that said Narcotics Anonymous on the front of them. They started flipping through the books, scratching words down on a piece of paper.

"Thursday is a day of recollection of our past behavior." Mary said.

"We read NA and AA and find ways to cope with life and our addictions." Mary walked over to the shelf and pulled down an Alcoholics Anonymous book. She flipped over a page and read it to me:

THE TWELVE STEPS TO RECOVERY:

1. We admit we are powerless over our addictions and our lives have become unmanageable.

2. We come to believe that a power greater than we could restore us to sanity.

3. We make a decision to turn our will and our lives over to the care of God as we understand him.

4. We make a searching and fearless moral inventory of ourselves.

5. We admit to ourselves and to another human being the exact nature of our wrongs.

6. We are entirely ready to have the defect removed.

7. We humbly ask God to remove our shortcomings.

8. We make a list of all persons we harmed and become willing to make amends to them all.

9. We make direct amends to such people whenever possible, except when to do so would injure them.

10. We continue to take personal inventory and when wrong promptly admit it.

11. We seek through prayer and meditation to improve our conscious contact with God.

12. We carry out all the Twelve Steps.

It sounded very religious to me.

"What we do, Abby," Mary told me proudly, "is work the Steps into our lives at The Village. Step One is what you'll be working on now, and once you're done with Step One and have shared your growth in the Group, you get to go off campus to the AA meetings. Every step you sincerely finish, you get more privileges." Mary sounded like some Bible-thumping fanatic. She was so excited and knew every detail.

I nodded my head, but I wanted to ask, "What about if you aren't an addict? Then what?" But I thought better of this, because Miss Strickler was watching us, as she tilted her chair back. She was always there!

Miss Strickler made me very uncomfortable. I was glad to hear that she would be leaving the next night for a three and a half day break. I didn't mind Miss Rossly though. She really didn't do much but follow Miss Strickler around, laugh at any jokes Miss Strickler made, and write things down.

I wanted Miss Strickler to stay away from me, so I tried to look remotely interested in the Twelve Steps Mary waved in front of my face.

Mary explained about each Step and what I had to do. Most of them sounded the same. Nothing with the word addiction and admitting addiction interested me at all. I wanted to choke Mary, the way she forced "addiction" on me like I was an addict. I could admit I was wild sometimes and ran away and had no respect for authority, but how did that fall under addiction? Maybe I was addicted to freedom.

"Have any questions?" Mary asked eagerly.

"Yeah, I do. Is there anything you can be addicted to besides drugs and alcohol?"

Mary's eyes opened wide, "Oh, I should have told you that. I'm sorry. Yes, actually Dannie and Shakira are addicted to . . . anger, while Candace has an addiction to cutting, and bulimia. I have substance abuse. There are so many addictions and dependent issues."

Although Mary explained this very clearly, I still didn't have the category of addiction that I so desperately wanted. I needed an addiction so I could get cured and then I could leave.

"Now what you do," she said, flipping the book to the Twelve Steps page again, "is work on Step One: write all the things you regret and how it affected your life." Then she gave me a pad and pencil.

Mary left me alone as she started working on her own Step Six. I stared at the blank piece of paper. I sat there a while. But then I did think about when I first met Enya and Sue. It was after I went to live with my dad and I wanted to make new friends. I joined up with them and they took me to the mall. My dad gave me all the money I wanted when I was thirteen. It was a way for him to feel responsible for being irresponsible. But we didn't go to shop. We went for the feeling we got when we walked out of the store with something we didn't pay for — we felt as if we had earned it in our own way. The excitement of getting away with it together ... the rush of releasing anger out onto the world.

I wrote this down and wondered if stealing was an addiction. *Is it normal to care so much about stealing from a store?*

When my stepmother came into my life, I remembered going

through her purse and taking half of the money, saying to myself it was my dad's anyway. Despite this, she still moved into our place. Once she did, I didn't stop stealing. I stole more. I stole her CDs, just to break them. I got so much pleasure out of this, but unlike stealing from the store, I got caught and punished. But it didn't matter. My dad had no right putting anyone or any rules in my life. My dad wasn't really a part of my life. That was the way I had felt then, but looking back on it, I realized I was a little odd.

Deep down I still had this anger about my dad, even though it was slowly going away. Unlike smoking weed, drinking, or having guys go down on me, I really enjoyed stealing and a part of me missed it. I was a very good thief. I never got caught stealing from stores.

I looked at the paper and continued to try to find more things I could be addicted to. When I thought of weed I thought of my ex-boyfriend, Ben. He was the town drug dealer. At the time, I thought this was really cool. He was like most suburban fuck-ups, thinking they are hard because the local school kicked them out for vandalism or something. Ben spent his free time (which was all his time) going from Hartford to West Hartford bringing back drugs and making contacts. My brother was one of his friends and liked the fact we were a couple because he got free weed out of it. My brother was nice to me when Ben was around.

I wasn't into Ben for the drugs, but I really liked the fact he gave me an allowance. The situation was really weird. I stole four hundred dollars from my dad and my dad called him saying he was a bad influence on me and threatened to call the cops. So Ben decided that I need some money so I wouldn't steal from my dad and he wouldn't get the cops on his ass. So, he gave me a hundred dollars a week, which was pretty good for not fucking him. The relationship ended pretty soon after though, and all together I only got two hundred dollars from him. I think not putting out had something to do with it.

The past is funny, sometimes you forget stories that seemed like such a big deal at the time. I looked back at this part of my past and it felt so long ago. It was almost a year.

In the middle of my flashback, Miss Strickler called for us to get into formation for lunch. Then lunch was silent because we stopped, without permission, to watch a deer. In a way I didn't mind. I didn't feel like talking. After lunch, instead of Group Therapy, we had Addiction Therapy.

Since I was new, I had to go first. I really didn't know what I was talking about.

"Today I listed all the things I did which I regret."

"Inventory is usually part of Step Four." Miss Strickler interrupted. "You're at the stage of seeing what's wrong with you. You do understand the difference?"

I nodded my head like I knew, not wanting to be in an argument with Miss Strickler. I really didn't have a clue about what she was saying.

"Well I thought a lot about my past and when I started doing bad things. For me, stealing was more of an issue, compared to drugs or alcohol."

Miss Strickler nodded her head. "So you are a kleptomaniac?"

"I don't know what that is. You mean a klepto?" Now, my regret was that I had brought up stealing with Miss Strickler. *Miss Strickler now thinks I'm a klepto, but I control myself when I steal. It's not an addiction. I'm not an addict, and even though I am fucked up sometimes, I wish they would get off my damn back!*

I decided Thursdays were bad days out in the Cabins. But until I finished Step One, I would have to sit in the Cabins while the rest of the Group had fun off campus.

TIME: 7:12 pm   **PATIENT NAME: Abigail Vona**

Group Treatment note: "It makes me feel sad that I don't feel like anyone else . . . it makes me feel sad that my father doesn't have 'wholeness' or values, it makes me feel depressed or stuck."

- Dr. K. Wisely

Day 113

I woke up excited because it was gardening day and Miss Strickler was leaving. I prayed that the replacement Staff was nothing like Miss Strickler. At breakfast, Miss Strickler asked me to sit and talk with her. I knew this was hardly a good thing, but I had absolutely no choice in the matter. She had some inner strength that showed through her face. I wondered if she was as strong as she presented herself or if it was a cover-up for something else. Maybe she felt inferior as a child and was an angry person. Whatever secrets she might hide within herself, I would never figure them out.

I sat next to her. She didn't talk though, just ate her Cocoa Puffs cereal. She refused to eat the cereal that was served in the cafeteria. Instead, she sat there like a queen, eating Cocoa Puffs. Any one of us would die to have a bite. She hovered over her bowl when she wasn't watching us. She never offered anyone a taste.

Miss Strickler placed a candy bar right in front of my plate and watched me look at it. It was a Snickers, and my mouth watered. It had been a long time since I had a candy bar, and Snickers was my favorite. This was the ultimate temptation. I watched Miss Strickler watch me. It was like she was testing me. Then I remembered the klepto thing. I knew kleptos were stealers but I didn't know much more than that. Miss Strickler pushed the candy bar closer to me.

She was taunting me with it. Hatred toward her filled my head like a thick fog. Then she just walked away and left me with the candy bar. I could have taken it, but I wasn't stupid. I just sat there playing with my food, not even looking at the small package of chocolate. She returned, just as breakfast was about to be over.

"So, you like Snickers?" she asked, practically pushing the candy bar onto my plate. She stared at me with her dark brown eyes and stuck her lips out, looking even meaner.

"I do."

She started eating her soggy Cocoa Puffs again, then sat back in her chair. She looked at me and the candy bar while she chewed her food.

"So why don't you take it, if you like it?"

I wondered if she was joking. It was so obvious. "Well, it's yours, Miss Strickler."

"That didn't stop you before. Do you only steal if you think you won't get caught?"

She hit the truth. *I only steal when I can get away with it. I never steal when someone might catch me.*

She suddenly snatched up the candy bar and put it in her pocket. I yearned for her to give it to me because I hadn't stolen it, but that didn't happen. *The greedy fat ass doesn't need the extra calories.*

After breakfast we walked to the farm site, about two miles away. We all had to put our heads down because the boys' clan passed us. I wanted to look but I didn't. The farm site was surrounded by a tall wooden fence. In front of the fence's gate stood another woman, who resembled an elephant that walked upright. What hair she had was black and curly. She was going bald and had more hair on her face than on the top of her head. A large Mickey Mouse shirt covered her large body.

"Good morning, Miss Grout," The Group shouted cheerfully.

Miss Rossly walked over to the strange woman and immersed herself in conversation in a low enough voice that I knew they were talking about us. *I wish I knew their secrets. If I knew, I would be out of here already.*

Miss Rossly opened the gate for us to go into the garden area. She led us to a field covered with small plants that appeared to be dead. "Now, Coyotes, you have to turn over the plants so they're mixed with the dirt. At the end of the day, I don't want to see any green." She then left us alone to plow the field with our shovels. Dannie went right to work, turning up the earth with all her strength. Then Mary joined in. Candace was the last to put any effort into the Group activity.

I enjoyed shoveling. It took my mind off what had happened earlier with Miss Strickler and the candy bar, but not totally.

Miss Rossly glided over, while Miss Grout sort of waddled. I didn't know what to think of these women. I went on looks. For some reason Miss Grout scared me.

"You're not going to introduce us to your new peer?" Miss Grout boomed at the girls, causing her belly to tremble with every word she let out.

Candace offered a pathetic lopsided smile, "Oh Miss Grout, this is Abby." Candace seemed genuinely glad to see Miss Grout.

"Well, Abby, why are you here?" Miss Grout asked. She was really an enormous woman.

I told her about all the stuff I did: marijuana, running away, drinking three times, and stealing.

"Stealing, I heard, is your main issue." Miss Grout said, confirming my suspicions of Miss Rossly talking about us.

"Yes, I would say that I enjoyed stealing a lot more than anything else I did." I prayed they didn't think I was a klepto, like Miss Strickler seemed to think.

"Have you stolen anything from this place?" Miss Rossly asked, making me feel at ease with her kind eyes. Now that Miss Strickler was gone, I felt good when she showed me any attention. I almost forgot that Miss Rossly had asked a question I could get in trouble for. *Did I steal here?* My mind drew a blank. There wasn't anything on STU *to* steal. But then two moments suddenly stuck out. One was when I took an extra muffin while passing out the food. The other was when I secretly switched a pillow, when we were changing our beds, because the other girl's was fluffier than mine.

I should have said "No," but for some reason, a sudden urge of honesty came over me.

"Well, I haven't stolen anything out in the Cabins, I mean, I've only been here for two days. But I did on STU."

Miss Rossly's blue eyes seemed to almost jut out of her head in complete surprise and Miss Grout's did, too. Even Candace looked stunned. Right when it came out of my mouth, I could have smacked myself. Good move.

"What did you steal on STU?" Miss Rossly asked in a soothing tone. I knew how pathetic it would sound, but anything you do on STU is very serious. "I stole a muffin and a pillow."

Miss Grout doubled over with laughter. She had to find a log to sit her large ass on because her whole body was rumbling out of control with hysteria. Miss Rossly tried to cover up a suppressed smile. Even Candace giggled. I realized how stupid I sounded, and I tried desperately to cover up my nervous laugh by playing with a stick. Miss Rossly became serious again, before I had enough control to wipe off my smile.

"Abby, you have a lot to learn, meaning we have lots to teach you. Do you think stealing is cute?"

My insides quivered at the thought of them teaching me. Their lessons were punishments and guilt trips and far from enjoyable.

"No, I don't think stealing is cute," I said.

"Well I think you're lying. If you have any guilt, you wouldn't have laughed. You would have felt guilty."

Miss Rossly was right. I had no guilt about stealing and was a little proud of it. I wasn't an addict, though. I had control. It was more of my identity. I didn't steal from just anyone. It was when I was mad, or felt like someone or something annoyed me, or when I didn't like or know the person.

I went back to shoveling and was glad I had something to take my mind off the present predicament. But I wasn't left alone. Miss Grout told the Group to watch me because I might steal and asked me to express myself when I had any impulse to steal.

The Group always announced their compulsions, especially Mary and Dannie. It was mostly like: "I have a compulsion to do drugs" or "I feel angry." I had absolutely no urge to steal anything, though. The only thing around me was dirt, plants, and manure, all of which I wanted to avoid, not take home with me.

After the garden site and before lunch, we played basketball. All of us just loved acting like little kids, it was contagious and a little bizarre. I thought that maybe it was because we'd all grown up so fast because of family problems or addictions that no one had a long enough childhood. Almost everyone just loved to regress to a time before we fucked up our lives. We were kids dying to be children.

That afternoon, I sat in the circle getting focused for Group Therapy. Dr. Wisely started with me. I knew he would probably be offended that I didn't "open up" about stealing on STU. I felt like a gladiator must have felt about to enter an arena, only I would die emotionally.

I started, "Well, I didn't tell you this but I stole some things on STU."

Dr. Wisely's eyebrow went up, he changed his position in his chair, and tilted his square glasses to see me better. "I stole a muffin when I was passing out food, and I stole a girl's pillow."

The Group covered up smiles, knowing it was not a good idea to laugh at me. Dr. Wisely looked dead serious.

"How did you steal a pillow?"

"Another girl and I were changing our beds, and when she wasn't looking, I switched pillows. Hers was fluffier and mine was sort of limp."

Shakira glared at me.

"It wasn't any of you guys."

Dr. Wisely shook his head, and I knew he was disappointed in me. I didn't want him to think badly of me. I wished I had never brought it up.

"How can we trust you in our Group?" Dannie asked, bringing up a pretty good question. It was like she was asking just to prove a point. *They really couldn't trust me. I never really cared for someone's trust until now.* I wanted them to trust me. I tried to think of a reason why they should trust me, but none came to mind. I just sat there thinking, *You can't trust me.*

Then Dr. Wisely said, "You can't trust her, not until she tells you when she wants to steal and realizes the importance and value of your trust."

I was the animal at the bottom of the totem pole.

TIME: 2:24 pm   **PATIENT NAME: Abigail Vona**

Group Treatment note: Patient expressed feeling "sad and frustrated." Patient stated, "I want to talk about my behavior this morning. I've been upset that I've been here a long time. I do feel like a failure. I was rude to staff. I feel sorry, but I think it's funny too. I see the

funny and the guilty. I don't know how to make the funny go away. The funny makes me feel better. Most of the bad things I've done are funny. My mother found them funny." Patient seemed to make excuses for herself. Patient seemed frustrated and tearful.

- Dr. K. Wisely

Day 117

Every little thing we did had a routine and too many rules. How to dress, how to undress, where clothes must go, how to wear your hair, when and how to brush your teeth, what was allowed and not allowed in the showers. Swearing was not allowed — that was a rule I had to get used to. But once I got used to it, I didn't swear and the idea of swearing didn't even come into my head. It was like the same thing with masturbation — you didn't do it because you couldn't. And if you don't masturbate, you lose your desire to masturbate — you stop even thinking about it.

When we were doing laundry in the morning, Miss Grout pulled me aside. Despite her rugged appearance, she was a really nice woman. "Abby, you look scared. Are you bothered by the Staff switch?"

I shook my head. I was far less scared of her than I was of Miss Strickler. "Or are you scared that we know you have a stealing problem?"

I was glad she said problem, instead of addiction, but I didn't think it was a problem.

"Now if you don't start telling us when you want to steal, we are going to assume that you are stealing or keeping things from us. It's as simple as that." Miss Grout had a strong but kind gaze that put me at ease.

I went back to my laundry and wondered if she meant to tell the

Group whenever I thought about stealing or whenever I considered it. *The truth is I think about it all the time!* For example, I wanted to steal Miss Grout's keys, but she was standing over them. Or sometimes I considered taking three packets of sugar for my cereal instead of two, just to get away with it. It's one of those things that you think about, but don't notice yourself thinking about. *Well, now I'm starting to notice just how much I think about it. And they have a point. I think about it a lot.*

TIME: 11:33 pm   **PATIENT NAME: Abigail Vona**

Milieu Treatment note: Patient became extremely tearful during vocational activities due to the reference of competence. Patient seemed to become irresponsible during vocational activities and was directed to Time Out due to unsafe behaviors and disregard to guidelines.

                                                      - T. Grout

TIME: 5:00 pm   **PATIENT NAME: Abigail Vona**

Group Treatment note: Patient called time to discuss her recent behavior. Patient stated that when she acts "dingy," she feels scattered and cannot think straight. These feelings lead her to feel hurried and somewhat panicked. Patient appeared receptive to staff input and made plans to explore possible triggers for her "dingy" behavior.

                                                    - Dr. K. Wisely

Day 120

I expressed a compulsion.

I had been having lots of conversations with Miss Grout about stealing. Miss Grout knew just how to deal with me, and the more I was around her, the more I respected her and the more emotionally attached I became. I wanted to tell her this but thought maybe I would sound like a stalking dyke, but that was absurd. No one would be sexually attracted to Miss Grout.

She said that only I could understand if my stealing was an addiction and I should express all my compulsions, no matter how stupid they were. I was glad that she was telling me up front about what I had to do.

So I told Miss Grout I thought of stealing her car keys. I don't think she expected that. She asked why and I told her I wanted to play with the funny looking ball that hung from them, which was only half the truth. The real reason I considered stealing them was if I was lucky, I could sneak away and take her car. Getting away with stealing her keys was unlikely, but running off unnoticed was impossible. And I was actually thinking of getting her keys, stealing her car, and escaping to Mexico. I didn't even know how to drive really. She laughed and gave me the keys to play with throughout breakfast.

Once I had the keys in my hands I didn't want to steal them anymore and I suddenly felt bad for having the thought in the first place. *Maybe I am fucked up.*

TIME: 5:13 pm   **PATIENT NAME: Abigail Vona**

Group Treatment note: Patient claims she feels badly because she is trying to earn trust from peers and staff and "stuff keeps happening to make you not trust me."
       - Dr. K. Wisely

Day 122

In the cabin as we were getting dressed, Miss Strickler got in my face, accusing me of taking her pen.

"Where is my pen?! Take off your sweater. Where did you hide it?"

About five minutes later, she was frisking me, convinced I had it. I went through an assortment of strange bends and pattings. I was stripped down to my underwear.

"Did you hide it in the cabin? The Group won't be pleased if we spend the whole afternoon tearing apart this place because you can't control your stealing."

I wondered what kind of pen it was. The only way I would steal a pen was if it was made of gold and diamonds, or if I really needed to write something down. I couldn't picture Miss Strickler carrying around a golden pen and I hadn't written anything down lately. *Why would I remotely want her pen?* I wanted to say this, but was afraid she might think I was being rude. So all I said was, "I don't have your pen."

Miss Rossly walked over as I was putting on my clothes. She had a cheap black and white pen.

"I found it, Miss Strickler. You dropped it."

Miss Strickler put the pen in her pocket. "I apologize, Abby, but now I hope you understand the value of trust."

I didn't understand why she didn't look for the pen first. I didn't understand why she cared about a two-cent pen anyway or why she thought I took it. And the last thing I wanted to understand was the value of trust. I was suddenly scared that the Staff didn't always know everything. How many false alarms would I be put through?

I started to cry. I wanted to tell her off, but saw no point. If I did I would go back to STU and never get out of here. I needed something or someone to shield me from all this shit. I wanted to run away from it all but I had no choice but to go through it. I was crying about something — what, I wasn't sure. I sat down on the floor and sobbed. I wanted to speak. But every word was consumed by choking. I had never cried like that before, and I tried to stop. I expected Miss Strickler or Miss Rossly to tell me to stop, but they just stood there. I felt like an idiot but I could do nothing but cry. Miss Strickler stood with me, while Miss Rossly took the Group to therapy.

Miss Strickler asked, "You know the Steps?"

I nodded my head.

"Well, you did the first one today. You admitted you are powerless and your life is unmanageable. Your stealing and the way you look at the world isn't working and you have to change it. To really change anything hurts, it's uncomfortable, it's like building muscle. It doesn't happen overnight."

I was definitely lost, frightened, and confused in my life. The meaning of powerless had just become too clear.

It wasn't until the Group was at the garden site that I was calm enough to join them. Miss Strickler asked if I wanted to speak about my experience with the pen. Knowing I needed to, I agreed. Before I knew it we were all circled at the garden site.

I told them what happened to Miss Strickler and what I felt, which was emptiness and fear. They all seemed truly interested in how I was feeling. I wasn't used to anyone truly caring about each other's feelings. The world I knew was a scary world, full of friendships that were based on what you got from each other. I was more than exposing everything.

"I understand where you're coming from, Abby," Rochelle said, after I told them how uncomfortable it was to tell them about my feelings. "I can relate, not wanting anybody to know who I was and how I truly feel. I wanted everyone to perceive me as a bad ass, long before I did coke. Now I'm trying to find myself, because all those years I wasted, looking for people's approval and hiding, and not becoming a true person."

For the first time, I saw part of myself in Rochelle and wondered if I kept doing stupid things that I might become more like Rochelle. *What if I get addicted to coke or heroin? What would I do for it?* The difference between Rochelle and me was that I happened to be lucky.

I had felt emotionally naked and I didn't think they would understand. I hadn't wanted anybody to know, because if they did, they would push me away. Instead my honesty brought them closer to me.

TIME: 2:01 pm   **PATIENT NAME: Abigail Vona**

Group Treatment note: Patient stated, "My mind goes blank, I don't have many feelings." Patient became extremely tearful at this time and stated, "I am not purposefully doing this stuff."

- Dr. K. Wisely

Chapter 2

ROPES

Day 123

The leaves were changing, turning bright orange, red, and brown. They reminded me of the beginning of school and that I was not home and that life was going on outside here and I was missing it.

Staff had to make a fire in the stove to keep us warm during the nights. It sucked not having a modern heating system and it was even worse that Miss Strickler kept reminding us that our wood stock was getting low, meaning we needed to chop more soon. If we ran out of wood and just didn't chop any more would the Staff let us freeze?

My fear of Miss Strickler didn't go away, but the more I was around her, the more I couldn't help but respect her. Although she had not searched me again, I still felt she didn't trust me. She was tough and gave me lots of Consequences. I had to do three pyramid tens for dropping a lantern three times. I kept on forgetting things too, like my garden tools at the site — so many times that Miss Strickler had me carry a log around to remind me to help improve my responsibility. The log wasn't working, though. I forgot that as well, which left me with more push-ups. Every day I must have done a thousand push-ups. I got so used to them that fifty felt like a breeze. My body was becoming mostly muscle. We had no mirrors or scales, so I prayed to God that I didn't resemble the muscle women on TV.

I really felt a part of the Group, but wished the Group was made up of just Dannie, Mary, Rochelle, and me. Candace and Shakira seemed to have burned out their sanity either with drugs, listening to Marilyn Manson, or acting like thugs.

At Group, Rochelle wanted to talk first about her family therapy. She was having what the Group called "break-throughs." Break-throughs could be good or bad, but they usually involved crying if it was Rochelle.

"I would like to talk about a traumatic memory from when I was a child," Rochelle said, hyperventilating in the chair from crying so hard. "When I was about three . . ." After this she had trouble getting any words out because she was so off in hysterics. Dr. Wisely had to give her a couple of minutes to calm down.

"Well . . . my mom and I lived alone in a one room apartment and I had to sleep in the living room." She paused to blow her nose really loud.

"My mom had a friend staying in her bedroom, so my mom and I shared the living room and at night, my mom would bring in her boyfriends, then they would then have sex right in front of me."

The whole room looked a little disgusted.

"Did you see anything?" asked Candace.

Rochelle nodded emphatically. "Yeah, I did . . . I saw everything."

"How many men did your mom have intercourse with in front of you, and how long did this go on?" asked Dr. Wisely.

Rochelle screwed up her face in concentration. "I don't know how many guys . . . maybe twelve? I was really young and it lasted once for a whole summer."

I couldn't believe her mom did something like that, or that

the men were okay with it. I never saw my parents have sex with anyone… let alone with each other, or even heard them do it. Something like that would have freaked the hell out of me. It seemed to really mess with Rochelle.

Then Mary revealed her secret identity. She told us how she once passed out drunk on her parents' deck after stumbling home from a party. Of course, she told her parents, who were worried sick all night and looking for her, that she had been out on the deck the whole night looking at the stars for her school project. The mother believed her. Her mother always thought the very best of Mary until she was caught fucking some guy in a parking lot at the convenience store.

"It was so horrible," Mary said in tears, "The look on my ma's face when she saw us." Mary's father wasn't as naïve after that, he would follow her around when he was off work to make sure she didn't do anything stupid.

Shakira, who was calm and sane for once, told us how she felt like the black sheep in her family and how they didn't understand why she needed to take her meds which made her feel bad, so she never took her meds when she was around her parents. She thought that if she had been on her meds, she would have never punched out the cop's windshield and chased that girl around with a baseball bat.

Candace went down memory lane too. She told us how her parents were coke-heads and she had lived with her grandmother. One time, she got angry at her grandmother and testified in court that her grandmother abused her physically. The innocent grandmother was given a restraining order so she couldn't see Candace. This worked out for Candace. She got to live with her coked-out parents and do whatever she wanted. It wasn't until she got in trouble with the law and was sent to court that her parents weren't allowed to see her. She was sent to live in a foster home before she finally gave a second thought to her dear granny. Candace devoted the rest of her time talking about how she missed her grandmother.

Miss Strickler said she would do her best to get rid of the restraining order and have visitation for Candace and her grandmother.

TIME: 5:34 pm   **PATIENT NAME: Abigail Vona**

Group Treatment note: Patient checked into session feeling "emotionally scared, sad, and depressed." She stated, "I'm confused because I don't want to steal anymore but it still makes me feel proud to have something even if I didn't work for it." Patient was very tearful as she spoke.

- Dr. K. Wisely

Day 124

At breakfast, I sat with Dannie. I watched as she drowned her food in white lumpy gravy. I stared.

"It's good!" she said, her mouth full of food.

It was disgusting.

"It's a southern thing."

Dannie and I talked about northern and southern food, and about restraints. I liked Dannie, despite the fact that she was a lesbian and looked weird. I felt at ease with her. She seemed to have changed since she beat up her family and came out here, or maybe I had changed. I couldn't tell.

When breakfast was over, we got into formation to go out to the ropes course. It was a long walk to the site. Shakira and Candace carried the Gott, ready to kill each other at any moment.

I was curious to see the ropes course. I pictured us swinging from ropes in a dense forest, but then realized they probably wouldn't trust us up high in trees, and they sure as hell wouldn't trust us with ropes.

We arrived, and my eyes lit up in utter awe. There in front of me was the most beautiful sight. There were ropes and wooden platforms in the trees and other strange wooden structures rose from the ground. But the beauty was behind it all — at one end, a river snaked below a huge, white, rock cliff. Birds in nests lay in the cracks or soared through the early morning sky. I wished that the cabin was out here.

"Well," Miss Rossly announced, "put the Gott by the tree and circle up right where y'all are standing."

"Today, you will exercise your Group skills," Miss Rossly said with a cheerful smile. I, on the other hand, wasn't cheerful about this. I looked at the Group — Dannie and Mary looked worried too.

Dannie and Mary were the only ones who went out of their way to make anything function. Rochelle pouted. I think Shakira, deep down, wanted to help, but didn't have the patience to calm herself down when other people pissed her off. And Candace, well the more I got to know her, the more I believed in Dr. Jekyll and Mr. Hyde — one minute she acted like an angel talking about feeling close to Jesus, and the next she did everything to piss people off and prayed to the devil. And people told me I was sometimes spacey and incompetent. We did not have a lot of Group skills.

"Okay," Miss Rossly went on, "we are going to do the team skis." She pointed to a clearing with two four-by-fours and six pieces of rope coming out of each piece of wood.

"This rock," she continued, pulling out a brightly painted green stone, "represents everything you left behind: drugs, sex, cutting, bulimia, stealing, prostitution. Well, the object is to stay away from this rock and go to the next rock on the skis. Yes, you heard me right. On the skis."

She pulled out a brightly colored pink rock. "This rock represents everything you want to go back to: good relationships with parents, NA and AA meetings, new friends, and school. Whatever will help you."

She went over to the clearing and put the green rock, representing bad things, next to the wood pieces. She then put the pink rock, representing good things, ten yards away from the bad rock.

"Now, each of you tell me three things you want to leave behind and three things you want when you leave this place. We'll start with you, Dannie." Miss Rossly pointed a finger at Dannie, who squirmed uncomfortably and started looking at the sky, as though in deep thought on what to say.

"Well," she began, "I want to leave my anger and frustration."

The funny thing about Dannie was that I never really saw her get angry. All she ever did was get red in the face and look constipated. She was probably like Mount Vesuvius, the volcano that can erupt but people forget it's anything more than a mountain for hiking. And the Group walked all over her too.

Miss Stickler called out, "Anger is a feeling, Dannie, it's just not going to go away. You need to learn to express it not suppress it. If you just avoid it, then it will come out as aggression."

Dannie nodded her head and took a breath. "Well, I want to control my anger." Miss Strickler seemed satisfied with this and let Dannie go on.

"I want to have a loving relationship with my family when I get out and be able to calm myself when I get really mad. That's all." Dannie looked at Rochelle.

Rochelle wanted to leave her pimp and get her GED. Candace

wanted to leave bulimia, cutting, anorexia, drugs, sex, and to go to church every day. Shakira sat down talking about how she wanted to leave drugs and sex and beating up people, while she glared at Candace, wanting to beat her up.

It was my turn. Suddenly, I didn't know what to say that would be good enough for Miss Strickler. *The thing is, my green stone in reality is my pink!* I wanted to go back to everything I left. I wanted my boyfriend, my friends, my fun, my parties, my clothes. Okay, I wanted to leave stealing, this was true, I didn't ever want to steal again.

"I want to leave disobeying my dad . . . and I want to go home with a good relationship with him. I also want to not steal." I looked around the circle for approval.

When the other girls finished, Miss Rossly explained, "All of you have to get on the two pieces of wood and move it along without getting off. You are allowed to grab the ropes. If one of you falls off the skis you go back to the green rock. The object of the course is to get to the pink rock."

Six people on wood skis? We couldn't set a table without a Consequence. This was going to be impossible.

"Now you can all start, and please talk to each other."

We looked at the pieces of wood. Shakira broke the silence, "Group, we need the strongest people in the back and in the front because we are going to be packed in." She was very enthusiastic, which was different for her. "The person in the middle has to have good balance because we only have seven pieces of rope. The back person has to tell us what is going on back there and the front person has to say, 'moving left foot' and 'moving right foot' as we go."

Miss Rossly interrupted. "Shakira, have you done this before?" It was a statement. Shakira knew everything about this exercise and probably every exercise in the ropes course. She had been in and out of The Village more than twice, not to mention placements in other treatment facilities.

"Yes."

Miss Rossly sighed. "Well, the purpose of this exercise is to have you work as a Group. How will you work as a Group when you tell them how to do the exercise?"

Shakira started to look angry again. Luckily she didn't explode.

Miss Rossly went on lecturing Shakira, which I thought was unfair because she was only trying to help.

"For your Consequence, the whole Group has to pull this off in silence. You're allowed to make hand signals, but that's it. Every time you talk, you have to go back to the beginning."

Before, I thought this would be impossible, now I knew we would be here, trying to do this, for the rest of our lives.

Dannie raised her hand. "Excuse me, Miss Rossly," Dannie said. "Can we have a Group to talk about what we are going to do before we start?"

Miss Rossly gave this some thought, then nodded her head in approval, "All right."

Dannie got excited again, "I say we do what Shakira said. Who thinks they can give good hand signals and is well-balanced?" Everyone in the Group stood there. They didn't seem to think this would work either.

"I can do all these things," Mary said, climbing up onto the wooden pieces.

"Okay, Rochelle, you get behind Mary," Dannie went on, "I won't take any rope because there are not enough pieces. Now Candace, come behind me. Abby, you too, and Shakira you go on the end."

Shakira, who was not paying attention, came out of her trance and just looked at all of us squished in on the wooden pieces.

"There's no room," she said.

This was true. The five of us barely fit. There was no room at all for Shakira. We scrunched more into each other. I wasn't appreciating Candace's body odor. She was far from hygienic.

I was at the end, and turned my head slightly to see the amount of room there was for Shakira. There was enough room now, but Shakira just stood back and shook her head. "Still not enough room," she said stubbornly.

Again we squashed more into each other before Shakira finally climbed on the pieces of wood and took her rope.

"Your silence starts now," Miss Rossly announced, and Mary put up three fingers to have us start to move. One finger down, two fingers down, then the last finger and all of us picked up the "ski" and placed it down. But just as we placed it down, Dannie lost her balance, and it created a chain reaction that caused Candace, Mary, and Shakira to fall.

We then switched order on the log. This time Shakira stepped up in the middle. And again we fell down. Shakira wouldn't get back on the four-by-fours again. "This isn't going to work!" she said with her arms flailing defiantly. All of our tempers were boiling over, but Shakira was outraged.

"Shakira, you shouldn't be complaining," Candace said, talking down to her. "It's because of you that we can't talk now. Can you please put in some effort?"

I wondered if Candace had a death wish. Shakira clenched her fists before snapping, "You fucking little bitch," making her way toward Candace. Shakira became her crazy witch-doctor self again and was about to jump on Candace and strangle her. But before she got there, Staff jumped between the two and struggled with Shakira's arms to hold her back.

"Dannie, blow the air horn!" Miss Strickler yelled, as Shakira got her arm back from Miss Rossly's grip and started punching her with it.

"Group, go to that tree and put your heads down!" Miss Strickler ordered, keeping a remarkable tone for the emergency at hand.

Dannie ran to the Staff's backpack and pulled out the red air horn. She pressed a button, and the little bottle made a huge, piercing noise.

It seemed like hours, but in about three minutes, cars and Staff came running, all to help control Shakira.

"Fuck you all. I want to kill y'all!" she screamed and screamed.

Then an ambulance arrived with a stretcher. Three nurses stepped out. One especially big nurse carried a syringe. The woman walked over to where eight Staff members held Shakira hard against the ground. The nurse then stuck the syringe into Shakira's ass. I knew that I wasn't supposed to watch the restraint but it was hard not to.

Shakira kept yelling and screaming. The nurse proceeded with the injection, ignoring the death threats and cursing.

"You fucking bitch, you're going to knock me out. I'll kill your mother-fucking . . . ahhh." The nurse had probably seen this all before. Shakira too. I certainly hadn't, not like this.

They put Shakira's limp body in the ambulance and drove off. I didn't know what to think. Staff just stood there, watching the ambulance drive down the road. Rochelle was sobbing, and Mary too. Dannie looked pissed off. Candace was pleased. A part of me wanted Shakira to never come back. Then we wouldn't have to worry about her attacking anyone, and our Group wouldn't be disciplined for stupid shit. But I was really scared for Shakira. Even though she was tough, she seemed helpless. I was scared for me too and I didn't even know why. *Where do girls go who fail out of here? Is there a worse place than this?*

TIME: 4:31 pm   PATIENT NAME: Abigail Vona

Milieu Treatment note: This patient seemed to be overly sensitive, becoming very tearful when a peer told her she didn't like an idea for a skit that this patient proposed. She has expressed no compulsions today. Patient participated in ropes course in the AM and seemed to participate well with her peers. She seemed to try to show leadership skills but appeared not to know how to be a leader.

- N. Strickler

Chapter 3

ROPES

Day 125

Miss Strickler told me I could go off campus with the rest of the Group that night. *It has been four months of being stuck at this place and now I am going to see the real world.* It didn't hit me that I was going to be with *the living* until I sat in the white van and we pulled out of The Village.

As we drove the hour to the AA meeting, we went over rules. We were paired up and had to stay within three feet of our buddy. We couldn't talk to anyone from the outside and if we were approached we had to break off the conversation. If anyone was there who we knew, we all had to leave. At least that was one thing that I didn't have to worry about. No one I knew would be caught dead in Tennessee, and my friends probably didn't even know AA and NA existed.

Since I was the least trusted, because I was new, I had to stay on three-foot with Miss Strickler. So, even though we were going off campus, it was far from freedom. Other "outside" rules were: no talking to men or being provocative, and no eating or drinking. There was also the big one: *No Trying To Run Away!* I had images of Candace pinned to the ground in a Wal-Mart by an entire police squad or I could see her screaming "child abuse" while Staff tried to make a restraint look normal in a parking lot.

Out beyond the confines of the car were woods, lakes, boat houses and people, ordinary people, walking and riding bikes. Looking at their freedom left me with a desire to do simple things and made me envy any life but the life I was living. *Every privilege I have, I have abused.* I was the living symbol of "give her an inch and she'll take a mile."

The road gradually went from country to suburb. More people filled the streets, not realizing how free they were. *Will I be like those people when I get my freedom? Will I cherish it or just forget the value of it?* I tried to un-depress myself by thinking of what I did have: health, youth . . . it stopped there. I wanted to say sanity, but I was at The Village so I didn't qualify.

We drove through a long tunnel opening onto streets. There were drunks, addicts, dealers, teenagers' and other people hanging out. It was a real city and this was not the very nice part. Of course, where do you expect to find an AA meeting?

A half-dressed woman carrying a brown paper bag stumbled into a liquor store. Usually, I wouldn't have thought twice about her or felt bad, I would have just seen it as her choice, but now I wondered how she got there, and thought of how sad and pathetic she was. I wondered if she was a prostitute, and that made me think of Rochelle.

We parked the van and paired off quietly. Miss Strickler eyed me closely. I wondered then if she could catch me if I ran. She was overweight and far from fit. I could see me running and Miss Strickler saying to Miss Rossly, "Catch her, don't let her get away!"

Miss Rossly on the other hand was fit, and sometimes did push-ups with us. I wished Miss Rossly spoke more. Maybe if she did, she would make Miss Strickler speak less. On the other hand, maybe we'd just have two Staff bitches. One bitch was enough for me.

I was glad the parking lot was empty. I had a sudden fear of how strangers would view me. I looked at what I was wearing, and felt my messy hair on my head and thought of my unplucked eyebrows. My own clothes were ten years out of style because Staff brought them for once. I never imagined walking in public and facing the world like *this*. What if I see a cute boy? How would people react to me? I was used to seeing eyes turn and sometimes stare when I walked into a room, being young and pretty. Now I was nothing like that.

As we walked toward the huge building, I tried to straighten my hair and fold my shirt. I didn't stop to think what Miss Strickler would say. She noticed everything and seemed to know what I was thinking. She sometimes assumed I was up to no good when I wasn't. That part seemed unfair. But, I gotta admit, most of the time she was right.

"Abby, it's sad you care so much about how people perceive you. That will be your downfall."

"Yes, Ma'am. I will work on that." I fixed my clothes back to normal.

"People need to see you for you, not what you are wearing. You need to find out who you are, not cover it up with pretty clothes and makeup, a fake ego of being a ditsy rebel who smokes weed."

Miss Strickler was right. And as much as I didn't want to face how truly shallow I was, I couldn't help it when my life story was laid out for me in a single sentence. She had a point. Why should I care? I walked into the building full of strangers. Fuck 'em.

We came in through the "exit only" door to avoid the crowd in front. Five hundred people were taking their seats in a circular auditorium. Being in a huge crowd like this was breathtaking for someone who had been in isolation for so long.

As we sat there, I tried not to look at people and just stared at the podium. Were people looking at me? How could I not care when I went home? It made me think of my mother's two cats.

It had been a hot summer and both cats had thick, long hair that made it an ideal place for ticks to hide. After a month of pulling out ticks, my mom took them to the vet to get shaved. They looked very funny and when the two cats saw each other for the first time, they hissed at each other. They weren't prepared to accept each other's appearance. Miss Strickler may have encouraged me, but she didn't take away the uncomfortable awkwardness. I felt like a shaved cat.

An ancient-looking man limped slowly up to the empty platform and gently grasped the mike. He shook a little, making me wonder if he was nervous or fucked up.

"Hi! I'm Andy and I'm an alcoholic."

"Hi, Andy," the crowd shouted.

"I've stayed clean and sober for about fifteen years and owe my life to this program. The speaker I'm introducing is an alcoholic and an addict. I've sponsored him for seven years. He achieved so much after hitting rock bottom. I'm proud to present him. Dr. Russell, will you come up and share your story?"

A tall handsome man rose from his seat and headed over to the old man with open arms ready to embrace him. The two men held each other. The old man looked at Dr. Russell like a son and his eyes went glassy. I thought their intense bond was strange. How could two men be so close without crossing the line to homosexuality? I knew that neither of these men were like that, though. I admired how they could care for each other so much. The old man took a seat as the younger handsome man stood on the podium, ready to speak.

"I'm Dr. Russell. I was thirteen when I took my first sip of beer but that's not when it started. I did have addictive qualities and showed them throughout my younger years. I remember shoveling everyone's driveway on my street to get money for a model airplane. I had to have it. It was so advanced that when I was able to buy it, and get it home, I couldn't put it together because I was too young to understand the instructions. So I threw it down the staircase. It broke. In that moment, I didn't see how I had just thrown away my savings. That's how I lived my life. Until I came to this program, I was working my ass off to throw my life away at bars, then on coke and prescription drugs, because I didn't have the means to understand how to live."

I didn't see where the airplane story fit into his addiction but it was entertaining.

"When I got to medical school, I drank large amounts of alcohol. I wasn't a social drinker. I was the kind of kid who had to out-drink everyone, until I passed out. Then it slowly became part of my life. To this day, I don't understand how I balanced alcoholism and med school, but I do remember struggling with graduating.

"My dad was so proud of my achievement that he let me take a year off to see the world. I remember going to Germany to tour the bars and taste the beer, France to sample the wine, Italy to see if bars were different from England's. I never saw a church, museum, or landmark; I lived at the pubs, bars, and clubs. I told myself, 'Well, I saw how the people truly live!'

"Then I made my way to Amsterdam. I had my first taste of acid and cocaine. Coke was amazing, and I promised myself I would always use it. On the plane going home, seven hours without my new love, coke, was torture."

I looked over at Rochelle. She had tears in her eyes. Her drug of choice was coke too.

"When I got home and settled down, first I found a coke dealer and then I got a job at a local hospital. I thought my life was set.

"One month into my addiction, I owed the dealer more money than I got from my job. After six months, I was twenty thousand dollars in debt. So I came up with a plan. I would write prescriptions for any drugs the dealer needed. This worked swell for a while. It was strange though, juggling my practice, my addiction, and my prescription writing. Although I had been good at functioning in my job, I was starting to slip up. One day, in trying to save someone, I made a serious mistake that led to this man's death. My world came crashing down. I got caught and it wasn't long before my fraudulent prescriptions were discovered. I was in jail in no time."

I squinted, looking more closely at Dr. Russell. He wasn't so handsome. Drugs must have affected his looks. He had bags under his eyes and his teeth were a little rotten.

"Jail is the best place to get off drugs. You have no choice but to quit and that's what I did. I went to AA meetings and found a solution to my problems and how to deal with my addiction. I owe my life to this program. When I got out of jail, I truly felt bad for everything I did when I was under the influence of drugs. I go to a meeting *every* day, sometimes two. It's my sanity. Thanks for letting me share."

The audience clapped and stood up to show their respect. I wondered if he was still in the medical profession — probably not, if he killed someone.

Before we left, the old man said a prayer. At the end, everyone in the crowd said the phrase, "One day at a time," like it was "Amen."

When we got into the bus, Rochelle was in tears.

"His story affected you, Rochelle?" Miss Strickler asked.

"Yeah. It got me thinking about my past and I realized I would have to face it again. I saw a man in the audience who looked drugged out. He was in the crowd. His eyes weren't even open. He reminded me of Joaquin. And then when Dr. Russell talked about all the coke, well, I just started thinking." Rochelle burst into tears all over again.

"The court orders people to AA meetings," Candace chimed in, "and they don't take it seriously. Some go there really high. My dad and mom used to be court-ordered there."

I could see Candace being court-ordered to an AA meeting and doing just as her parents did. If I was going there, and if I took the program seriously, I would try to kick those people out.

"I'll be honest," Rochelle said, "I miss coke. I miss Joaquin, but I hate myself for that and can't stand how I feel. I know I'm not ready to face it yet. I don't think I'll ever be able to face it." She was very upset. I felt sorry for her but I was proud and surprised by her honesty. I didn't want Rochelle to go back to being "super-ghetto-coke-head-whore." I liked her as a dramatic free spirit who sometimes acted like a child. I hoped that Joaquin got shot before Rochelle returned home. That would be a lot easier for her.

TIME: 5:46 pm   **PATIENT NAME: Abigail Vona**

Group Treatment note: This patient checked into this session feeling "depressed, frustrated and withdrawn." Patient stated, "I thought it would be cool to take my brother to an AA meeting. But, knowing my brother, he would probably bring a bag of weed."

- Dr. K. Wisely

Day 127

I stood inside an ancient-looking shed. Everywhere inside were axes, hammers, saws, and other strange tools I didn't even know existed.

There were axe-like looking things called mauls hanging on the walls by huge nails. On the ceiling hung five large saws with their sharp blades facing up. They were the length of a large man and had a handlebar at each end. I didn't feel safe standing under them, to tell the truth, and I had a sudden fear that an earthquake might hit, making them fall and killing us. Dannie looked fearless though as she reached to pull one down.

"Abby, can you get the other side?"

I walked over to help her out, and we pulled down one of the enormous saws. The day was going to be dedicated to chopping wood so we could heat our cabin during the winter.

We took the trail in the opposite direction of the Cabins. I had never been this way before. It wasn't long before we came to a clearing, with hundreds of logs in different shapes and sizes. I couldn't help but recall STU. On STU, they didn't even trust me with plastic forks or let me take showers in private. Now, I was carrying a saber-toothed saw that I could easily use to kill myself or to severely fuck up Staff. I pictured myself holding the large saw to my neck and demanding my freedom, "I'll saw myself, I swear." But I didn't have the guts, and they would probably restrain me before I could put the plan into action. *Why am I still thinking these things?*

Mary took small pieces of logs that seemed to be cut from larger ones. They were around two to three feet long. Rochelle and Candace took their massive saw over to a log that was lofted from the ground by two pieces of wood.

I was glad to be working with Dannie. I mean, I didn't really want to be joined together by a huge saw with Candace or Rochelle. And thank God Shakira wasn't here for this, it would probably be a massacre.

Rochelle and Candace didn't seem to be doing well, though. The saw kept moving out of place, and Candace kept on telling Rochelle she wasn't doing it right.

Dannie coached me, "You have to start slowly, moving the blade back and forth. Then use more pressure once the saw has formed a cut. You got it, Abby?"

I nodded. Dannie and I made our way to a log near Rochelle and Candace. They were still arguing, but the saw was starting to leave its mark in the thick trunk of wood. We put our large saw over the log, ready to saw through it. Dannie slowly pulled, and then I pulled.

"Slowly, slowly, not too much pressure." Dannie instructed, while the saw slowly moved through the bark of the giant log. "That's good. Pull, not push."

I got the hang of it and the saw dug deeper, spouting fresh sawdust from both sides of the blade. We started pulling faster and faster as the blade went into the tree deeper and deeper. By the time we were halfway through the log, I started to lose my breath. I wanted to stop but I really wanted to finish this and cut the log. I knew I would feel weak-willed if I gave up.

It wasn't until about fifteen minutes of sawing that we were almost finished. The log finally fell to the ground in pieces, and I was drained of energy. Cold sweat ran down my face. Dannie looked exhausted, too.

"Good job," she said with a smile. "You're going to be a good cross-sawer."

I was really starting to like and admire Dannie. She had an ability to juggle more than one chore with a kind of powerful grace. She reminded me of one of those big plough horses. She was able to do large amounts of work and still run the Group. Her large body pranced around the cabin, taking care of garbage, the Gott, and getting the backpacks filled with things we needed. She even told Candace to stop making petty Confronts. I didn't think of her anymore as a scary, hick-ass lesbian, but a kind, strong, friendly girl with some anger problems. I thought that maybe Dannie was like the Incredible Hulk, without the turning-green part. A good person who you sort of waited for to snap and go nuts. But she never did, she never made the transformation. But you knew that maybe she could, because she was here for that reason.

I looked over at Rochelle and Candace. They were sitting down on the log they were supposed to be sawing, sipping water, while their saw wasn't even halfway through. I felt proud of my accomplishment.

"Now we can trade out with Mary and maul this piece of wood." I watched Mary give a circling swing with the maul around her body, sort of like a golfer's stroke, then hitting a piece of wood, causing it to splinter.

"Mary, can you trade with Abby and me?"

Mary put her maul on the ground and looked disappointed, but said, "Sure," in a forced pleasant way. Miss Strickler was her buddy that day so she didn't have a choice.

Dannie led me over to the maul. I couldn't help but notice Candace beating the hell out of her piece of wood, and thinking of a crazed axe murderer. I didn't trust her with that tool and was shocked Miss Strickler did.

Dannie picked up her maul and gestured for me to do the same. I felt safer being around Candace now that I had a weapon too.

"What you do is swing the maul over your head, and hit it right in the center of the log." Dannie then swung her maul at the log, which split down the center but not all the way.

"You got it? Have any questions?" Dannie asked.

"Nope, I think I can handle it," I said, lifting the maul to the piece of wood Mary had been working on. I stood there holding the maul, getting used to its weight and feel before I swung it over my head with all my might. To my amazement, it landed smack in the center of the wood, six inches in, and the two pieces separated.

"Good, good!" Dannie laughed. "You're going to be good at this, too. Now finish it off."

I took another swing but this time got carried away with my sudden success. The maul hit the middle of the log and stuck in halfway, leaving me with a piece of wood wedged in my finger. The splinter was big enough for me to pull out. I put the maul down.

Dannie noticed. "You okay? Got a splinter? I'm sorry. It happens sometimes. The mauls are old and falling apart. They sometimes give you those when you slide your hand down the handle too quickly."

I pulled the piece of wood out of my finger.

"Blood!" Dannie said in alarm. She backed away, as if bleeding was another rule not to break.

"Staff, Abby is bleeding." Dannie backed away from me. "Abby, when a Group member bleeds, we have to stay three feet away. It's not you, that's the rule. It's for medical precaution."

Miss Strickler and Miss Rossly quickly came toward me with gloves on and Band-Aids. They disinfected my wound, gave me a Band-Aid and told me to sit down by them. At first I was freaked out by all this. Then it hit me, they really had to worry about this here. I mean they had to worry about AIDS and other diseases.

"It's not a punishment." Miss Rossly told me. I slouched down beside her.

"Anyway," Miss Strickler said — she always had to have the last word — "you need to get focused for Family Therapy. You get picked up in ten minutes."

A few minutes later, a bright yellow Volkswagen Beetle pulled up from a side road. Out stepped Miss Fawn.

I was a little disappointed she came when I was about to maul some more. I had almost forgotten about Family Therapy. I wanted to tell my dad about chopping wood and sawing the log. Here I was a thousand miles away and I was becoming closer to my dad. For the first time in my life, I actually thought about him as a person, not just a bank account, provider of my clothes, and pain in my ass. I really looked forward to talking with him.

I sat in Miss Fawn's office and picked up the phone eagerly, waiting as she dialed his number.

"How's Coyote Clan, Abby? Are you excited about Family Therapy?" she asked, overly enthusiastic as usual. She reminded me of a talk show host who acted like she cared, just to milk you for all the dirt you were hiding.

Just then a voice answered. It was a woman's voice. A voice that made the veins throb in my neck.

"Hello!" the woman said. "Hello?"

It was Judy, my stepmother, of all people. I wasn't the only one who was shocked. Miss Fawn's mouth was wide open.

"Is Dr. Vona there?" Miss Fawn gestured for me to put down the phone.

I quickly hung it up, furious. Judy's voice had pierced my ears, making my head feel like it was about to blow up in pure rage. How could he let her do that?! What was my dad thinking, having her pick up the phone?!

And now I questioned if his plan all along was to stick me in this place forever and never let me out until I was eighteen, when he didn't have to support me anymore. He could then be free to play around on a beach somewhere with my stepmother. It was like they were trying to keep me here!

For the first time in my life, I was glad I was at The Village, so I wouldn't get a life sentence for killing both of them.

I put my head down in my lap and listened to Miss Fawn, but Miss Fawn just sat there, waiting to speak to my dad. It was a while before she spoke.

"Dr. Vona, oh good! Was that Judy? Oh . . . well, I thought we weren't going to start therapy with her for another month."

I didn't need to hear my dad speak to know what he was saying. I was starting Family Therapy with Judy! *To think that I might be starting Family Therapy with her before my own mother!* This wasn't fair.

Miss Fawn looked flustered. "Well, no. Actually I don't think that's all right. It's in Abby's best interest not to have to deal with all of this now. We will start Family Therapy in a month. Please, can you have her leave?"

I knew Judy had insisted on butting into my life, just as she always did. And my dad was too much of a pussy to say no. I was glad Miss Fawn insisted on having her leave. *When I do go home, I wish I could bring Miss Fawn with me to tell my stepmother and father off. I was glad that somebody knew I wasn't crazy here.*

The thing I was confused about was why now, when she had gotten her way at last, would she try to come back into my life? *There are five states between the two of us and no visitation. She would like nothing better than to taunt me with the fact that she won, the fact that I have no freedom anymore.*

I wished my mom was here to put Judy in her place. Suddenly I really missed my mom, but they don't like my mom here because she doesn't have custody . . . or money.

"Abby," Miss Fawn said, "you can pick up the phone. Your dad's the only one we will talk to today."

I picked up the phone and asked him why Judy was there. He said she couldn't wait to talk to me. I told him I hated her and never wanted to see or hear from her. And he told me to give her another chance. "You only hate her because your mom hates her, your mother never liked any of my girlfriends." My dad did have a point.

Then, with much persuasion from Miss Fawn, I agreed to speak with Judy in a month and not be rude. And I forgave my dad for his stupidity. We talked about the Cabins for the last two minutes of the therapy session.

I rode back in Miss Fawn's car, and even though I hadn't heard music for months I didn't care that Miss Fawn played Led Zeppelin.

We all sat down on the floor of the cabin, except for Staff. Just as we put our heads down to get focused, Dr. Wisely walked through the door, "Hello, Coyotes."

Dr. Wisely had not sat down when I blurted, "I want to express myself. I had Family Therapy today and I was expecting my dad to pick up the phone and instead my stepmother did. See, I didn't tell you all this, but I hate my stepmother and we never talk."

Dr. Wisely's eyes rolled. "Well, Coyotes, Abby hates her stepmother and unlike all of you, I have heard the story. Basically, Abby's stepmother is not a perfect woman. They had their issues and Abby seems to blame her stepmother for everything that goes wrong in her life."

I tried to speak up, describing the time she threw me into the fence at the fair or the time she didn't buy me a birthday present, but he gave me no room to talk.

"Don't get me wrong, Abby. She did do some messed-up things, but you need to grow up, whether she has or hasn't. You need to take some responsibility for yourself. Now I advise you to suck it up and tell the Group something about *you*, not your stepmother."

I didn't want to take in what he was saying, and I didn't want to admit he might be right, even in my mind. I just wanted to sit there, not saying a word, while they all stared at me. Then I thought about STU and the hard beds and fluorescent lights that I might have to go back to. I quickly searched my mind for something I could tell them . . . my so-called issues.

"Tell us about your mother and you, Abby," Dr. Wisely said. "Tell us, who was the first person to give you a cigarette?"

This was a funny question. I never really smoked cigarettes, never had a problem with them, so the subject never came up. I didn't want to answer him if the story behind it sounded worse than what it was.

"My mom." Everyone looked at me.

"Why did you keep that from us?" Dannie asked as if it was a dark secret.

"She gave us the cigarettes to show us that they weren't anything special." I knew that Dr. Wisely didn't see it that way. My mom is just a free spirit.

"Who is 'we'?" Dr. Wisely asked.

"My brother and me."

"Does he smoke?"

I nodded.

"When did he start smoking?"

"Right after my mom gave us the cigarettes he would steal my mom's for years."

"And tell us, Abby, did your mom allow you and your brother to smoke weed at her house?"

I nodded and realized that Dr. Wisely and my dad probably had a private chat. "The first time I smoked pot was under her roof when I was living with her. She cooked for us when my brother and I got the munchies. She said that it's better to experiment now than later."

"Do you think your mom is a good person for you to be around?" Dr. Wisely asked the uncomfortable question.

I wanted to say that because she's my mom it shouldn't matter but I had a feeling that was not the answer he wanted to hear. "I don't know." I didn't know!

My head was a little numb. It was Mary's turn. I didn't pay any attention to her because she was going on and on about a dream with baby toys. I was thinking about my own problems

Then Mary said something that caught my ear.

"I know now what the dream meant, it all makes sense, it's all related . . . to my abortion."

I pulled out of my self-pity and tried to figure out what Mary was talking about.

"Now that I'm over it, well, sort of over it, I wish I never snuck out that night, I wish I never had . . . sex with him. He didn't care, he didn't care enough to let me heal." She was now very upset.

Mary was consumed by this thing. I didn't know the details and this story wasn't something I could relate to, but I had never seen her like this before. She was always cheery for the most part.

"I tell myself I wasn't ready and I wasn't. I just couldn't take care of a baby. Look at me, I'm here." She paused and her thoughts went to some other place. "When I told my mom and dad they took it well. They told me to forget about it, but I can't. My dreams, my daydreams, bring it back and back." She sobbed. "Every time I have my period I think about it more. If I had stayed away I would have never gotten pregnant, never gotten an abortion, never gotten infected, and I would still be able to have kids, but I can't now!"

Tears ran down her face, but she didn't bother to wipe them away.

TIME: 9:09 pm　　　　　　　　　　**PATIENT NAME: Abigail Vona**

Milieu Treatment note: Patient was sent to Time Out in the PM for unsafe and disrespectful behavior, which seemed to be a result of very unaware and dingy behavior. While in Time Out she appeared to behave in a very attention-seeking manner, as shown by loud crying and speaking out to staff at inappropriate times. Patient was placed in this Time Out for horseplay in the bathhouse, which resulted in the destruction of a sink and possible danger to herself, staff and peers.

- N. Strickler

Chapter 4

DICTIONARY

Day 131

M iss Strickler announced that a new girl was coming to the Coyotes, "Some of you know her. It's Ally."

Candace made a face. "Ally? I thought she left this place three months ago." She looked almost angry that Ally was back at The Village. Candace, who was also a second-timer, then told us that she had been Ally's peer in the very same cabin with the same Staff months before. "Ally, she's been here and to about thirty other placements across the country with me before this place, before she ran away."

Just then Ally came in with Miss Rossly. Ally was thin right down to the bones, and had straggly mousy brown hair that hung limply to her shoulders, framing a white rigid face. Her lips were thin lines on a large mouth. She looked sweet enough. Her green eyes contrasted with the white part that was all bloodshot. She looked totally drained of life.

A few minutes later we started Group Therapy and Ally introduced herself.

"Hi everyone, my name's Ally. This is my second time at The Village." She spoke in the harshest southern accent I'd ever heard. "I'm here for a lot of things actually, like smoking . . ." Her voice started to catch, like something was stuck in her throat. "Drinking and running away from my placement . . ." Her voice choked more and more as she tried harder and harder to fight back tears.

"I was doing good at my placement and then . . ." She paused to rub her eyes.

"But my ma, see, we have a really unhealthy relationship." The words became hard to hear through her thick accent and choking voice. The tears she both cried and tried to hold back. Miss Rossly seemed to be holding back tears too. Ally kept looking at Miss Strickler though.

"Ma and I do things together. I ran back to her and her boyfriend, and got into loads of trouble. The same trouble I was in before, only it seemed a whole lot worse." Ally settled down.

Miss Strickler said, "We are really interested in your mother and would like to hear about why you decided to take off from your placement."

"Well, I was there for two weeks and then one day I heard my mom was looking for me so I went to see her. I was living with another family, a really nice family. It's just they weren't my family."

"Would you say you take care of your mother? Do you feel she needs you?" asked Miss Strickler.

Ally's eyes got glassy again. "She does need me. When I got to her, she was all a mess. She can't live alone without me."

Rochelle looked confused. "Is she handicapped?"

Miss Strickler gave a laugh. Ally who didn't see the humor, got angry. "No, she just can't handle herself . . . mentally."

"Can you be more specific?" prodded Miss Strickler. Miss Strickler knew all the details on everyone.

"Well, when I came back, as I said, she was a mess; just a wreck. Her hair seemed to be stuck in tangles and her teeth were really messed up. She looked thin, way too thin. She didn't have a home and was living with Samuel, a crack dealer, for an exchange of various things, like sex and selling his drugs. My mom never had a real job."

When Ally brought up sex in exchange for favors, Rochelle got upset.

"I came back to be with her and she got better. We both got jobs and rented a small apartment."

Something about Ally's story made me suddenly feel uncomfortable. I couldn't help but see the parallels between her mom and mine. *Ally's mom acts like my mom.*

"What jobs did you two get?" Candace asked.

Ally sighed, "We worked at a liquor store and sold weed to make ends meet."

Although being a drug dealer and working in a liquor store when you are under age is probably better than selling yourself and living with the local crack dealer, it is not exactly something to brag about.

Ally's mom was a prostitute and a cocaine addict. Ally's dad was her pimp. Ally first had sex at age eleven. She also had many problems with abusing cocaine, heroin, and marijuana. She mentioned how her mom used to smuggle her drugs in previous treatments she went to. "She would make me peanut butter sandwiches and put the marijuana in a plastic bag in the middle of the sandwich," confessed Ally. You could see it on her face that she felt as though she was betraying her mom by even telling the story. Her mom gave her drugs so freely, they might as well have been vitamins or medication.

Ally only attended five years of school, and ran away from twenty-eight Group homes and seven institutions. This place was the only one she didn't run from. I assumed it was pretty hard to run from The Village. She was a very normal girl who just had the most fucked up past.

She stopped, looked around the Group and asked, "Who else calls time? It's my first day here, so I'm not going to take up all your time."

Candace went next. "I'm so fed up with things. Not just on the unit but in my life, my whole life! I'm not allowed to go to church here and be one with my savior! I can't handle any of this." Candace was soon interrupted by Ally's maniacal laughter.

"The only reason your life is unmanageable, Candace, is because you make it that way," Ally said firmly. Candace just stared at her, not having a clue what to say. Ally had known Candace for months and knew all her bullshit.

"You act so foolish and don't care about anybody. How do you expect people to care about you when you treat them like crap and 'worship' the devil…or Jesus this week."

What Ally said was so true. I had never heard someone be so straightforward, especially in this place. I looked over at Staff who just nodded their heads with smiles of approval for Ally.

"Ally," Miss Strickler said with a curled smile, "your honesty is so refreshing. I can tell you've gone through this program before." Ally didn't take this as a compliment because she slumped in her chair, probably embarrassed that she had to come back here.

"Ally, we are sorry," said Miss Rossly. "We should have known that you would never leave your mom, even when you're sacrificing everything."

Later that morning I saw Ally walk over to Miss Strickler. "You mad at me, Miss Strickler?" She reminded me of how a terrified dog must look before his abusive master hits him. That was what it felt like when you disappointed Miss Strickler.

"How can I be mad, Ally? It's your life you're ruining, but I'm extremely disappointed."

Miss Strickler turned to the group. "Ally knows enough of the rules and won't be obligated to be on grace or three-foot. You all right with that, Ally?"

Ally nodded, then stepped into formation and knew right where to go.

At the garden site, Ally worked hard, digging and plowing. She fit in with the Group. She knew all the rules, probably better than the rest of us combined. Ally seemed to have a good influence on Candace too, who actually shoveled and worked harder herself now. Ally had a natural way of nurturing troubled people after spending so many years caring for her crack-head mother.

Ally helped Dannie put away the shovels, giving Dannie a deserved break from being the Group's caretaker. Miss Strickler noticed Ally's immediate leadership too, but didn't view it in the same light. "Ally, I see you picked up where you left off. This time I hope you actually learn something you can use in your life."

Ally's eyes were over-squeezed oranges, dry and pulpy with nothing left. She was the orphan girl you wanted to bring home and take care of, not like the rest of us spoiled shits. Something about her you couldn't help but respect but at the same time feel sorry for. God gave her a terrible life and she just tried to stay alive — I was given wealth and all I did was try to find trouble.

I think if Ally was adopted by the richest, happiest family in the world she would still run away to her drug-addict prostitute of a mom. I understood how she couldn't help it.

TIME: 5:14 pm   **PATIENT NAME: Abigail Vona**

Group Treatment note: Patient expressed, "I feel better. I am not acting dingy." Abigail described having felt scattered, with her thoughts not "together," or realistic, and having played the victim. Patient stated, "I am acting dingy to make others take care of me."

- Dr. K. Wisely

Day 134

I had a dream about Matt. I was back from The Village and lived like I used to live. I slept over at Matt's house whenever I wanted, ran off without permission, smoked weed, and despite my love for Matt I became out of control and hopeless about life. Somehow we wound up far away from my family. We were homeless and lived in a cardboard box. He started shooting up and I tried it too and also wanted more. Then I became afraid of him. He became really scary. I wanted to leave him but I was too weak to run. He started hitting me, and when I finally decided to run, he chased me. The rest of the dream was me running from him.

I woke up in the darkness — the dream was fucking weird. It was like I needed Matt and couldn't leave him for some reason. But he was bad for me. He was killing me inside and out and then at the end he really tried to actually kill me.

My bad mood grew as the day went on. I couldn't shake the dream. Miss Strickler seemed to become suspicious of me again, like she was on a "not liking me" streak. The day was spent chopping wood. My anger doubled as I swung the maul really hard into pieces of wood, imagining it to be Miss Strickler's head.

Miss Strickler took a break from sitting on her ass, drinking soda, and started showing us how to do things. She walked over to me and watched me swing the maul. "No, no, no, you need to have rhythm and not put so much strength into it. If you learn to do it right and cut enough wood, you could become a 'bear.'"

The Village had a stupid classification system like the Girl Scouts: mouse, bear, eagle, and buffalo. Everyone who came in was a mouse. A mouse meant you got no privileges and almost everyone was a mouse. If you did good things you became a bear and that meant you could drink coffee and wear a ring. An eagle meant you could wear light makeup, a necklace, and you could walk alone. No one became an eagle. And a buffalo could go and do as she pleased at The Village. As far as I know, no one in the history of The Village became a buffalo ever. No one cared about these badges and no one moved beyond "mouse."

Miss Stricker walked over and grabbed the maul from me. "Like this, I'll show you." Miss Strickler swung the maul, letting gravity pull it down and split the piece of wood that I was struggling with. "Now you try."

She gave the maul back to me and stood over my shoulder, waiting for me to swing. I didn't like being watched and wanted her to leave me alone, but she hung over me like a vulture. Distracted by her, I swung the maul, missing the wood entirely. Instead it hit the gravel, sending a stone right into her face. She grabbed her mouth and fell to her knees.

I came over to her. "Miss Strickler, I'm sorry. I didn't mean to." I couldn't believe my bad luck. *Now I know I'm going to be in trouble.*

"Please, just sit over there," she directed me under a tree with the hand that wasn't holding her bleeding mouth. When the crisis was over and Miss Strickler's fat lip was bandaged up, I had to sit under the tree, with three pieces of paper and write about how I was unsafe and irresponsible. The paper I had to write wasn't the extent of my Consequence — I couldn't do any wood chopping for the next four wood-gathering days, meaning I had to saw, which wasn't as much fun. I don't know what was below a "mouse" but that's what I was now to Miss Strickler. Maybe a mosquito.

TIME: 2:30 pm   **PATIENT NAME: Abigail Vona**

Milieu Treatment note: Patient is on a dingy intervention, and she was very dingy at times. Patient became extremely tearful with

uncontrollable sobbing. Patient stated, "I'm just a screw-up. I don't think I can stop it." Patient continued to cry for over an hour but she seemed to calm herself.

-N. Strickler

Day 135

The next morning I wrote my three pages on how to improve my wood chopping skills. Writing was torture for me. I couldn't spell and even had problems reading. In my school, back home, I wasn't in the mainstream classes. As a dyslexic, I was put in special-ed classes where they gave C's for doing nothing.

I would always be dyslexic, a word impossible for me to even spell, along with most others. This was something I struggled with throughout my life, and always would. And though it was no excuse, it must have contributed to some of my problems. Dyslexia made me look for ways to cheat all during school. It wasn't like I was looking at someone else's paper or anything — I just had to cope with learning differently than others. I had to find a way around everything.

Like when we had a spelling bee. I got the highest score in the school during the first round. We were given multiple choice questions, and I could just tell if a word was spelled right, or not, just by how it looked. I had a really good visual memory.

So suddenly all these teachers thought I was a spelling genius, but then I had to get up for the second round in front of the whole school. And I was supposed to spell these words aloud from what they read out to me. I totally broke down. Everyone in the audience was expecting me to screw up and I did. I couldn't see the letters in my head and read them back one by one. They got all confused like always. So everyone thought I was some moron who had cheated on my test. As if I wanted to be in some spelling bee in the first place.

I guess for me reading was kind of like trying to talk for a stuttering person. You don't have the time to read like everyone else. So you gotta find ways of getting the answer without doing the work. I know it sounds retarded but it's how I've always been.

It's why most dyslexics get in trouble in school. You find ways to cheat, then work less, then get lazy and then people think you're a fuck up, so you start being a fuck up. But what do teachers know? Einstein was dyslexic.

I handed the pieces of paper to Miss Strickler, and she circled about fifteen words on each page.

"All of these words are spelled totally wrong. Now, I want you to rewrite this paper with all the words spelled correctly. The dictionary is on the shelf."

I wanted to remind Miss Strickler that I was dyslexic, but it was just no use with her.

I had rarely used a dictionary, and I always asked for spelling on words I didn't know. I gave Miss Strickler the paper again.

"You spelled this wrong, this wrong, and that's used incorrectly."

I spent part of dinner and my free time before showers trying to spell and rewrite once more. I gave her the paper several times, and every time Miss Strickler circled more and more. It was so incredibly frustrating.

I hated spelling more than I hated this place. I had to restrain myself from tearing up the whole paper.

When she accepted the paper, Miss Strickler said, "Your spelling is atrocious. Do you know how to even use that thing?" She pointed at the dictionary.

"Yes, but I'm a little rusty."

"Miss Rossly and I have decided you need to improve your spelling so we came up with a solution. You're the new spelling helper."

I didn't like the sound of "spelling helper."

"You will carry the dictionary wherever you go. Whenever one of your peers wants to know how to spell something, you have to look up the word and tell them. I will announce this to the Group."

This was bad. They called this an "intervention," when one girl is singled out for a chore or responsibility outside the Group. It was the worst kind of Consequence.

The next few days with Miss Strickler and Miss Rossly were awful. They had me look up words, spell them out loud, then read off the meaning. Some of the girls liked to see me suffer, so they had lots of spelling questions too. Even in the porta line they would ask for spellings just so they could see me juggle holding the line rope and reading the dictionary.

TIME: 8:02 pm   **PATIENT NAME: Abigail Vona**

Group Treatment note: Patient expressed, "I think of how I'm going to be when I get out of here. It doesn't bother me that I stole stuff, but it does that people might think bad things about me."

– Dr. K. Wisely

Day 140

I was off dictionary patrol for a change, but I still had to write. I was on Step Four — an inventory of every single time I stole, lied, or cheated that I could remember. This was very time-consuming and took me weeks to accomplish.

I wrote down all the times I could think of when I stole. One incident stuck out in my head, and I couldn't say I wouldn't be tempted to do it again when I got out. During the late spring, my friends and I would go out to the town park after a late party. The park was famous for its rose garden. People from the town would volunteer to take care of the incredible gardens so that the flowers were amazing.

We would go to the park just before dawn with enormous garbage bags and clippers. And then we would fill up entire garbage bags with the best and most rare flowers the park had to offer. We would clip and steal hundreds if not thousands. When I came home, my room would look like a funeral parlor. To my mind, stealing from the community didn't even feel like stealing.

At dinner, a middle-aged man and a woman entered the dining hall. The man wore a faded leather jacket that looked as though it was soaked in dirt to get its color. He looked dirty too, and the woman had terrible posture and slouched to a 135-degree angle. Homely was an understatement for her looks and she had alligator-dry skin. The couple looked like they lived in the swamp. I knew they were Dannie's parents.

She ran over to her parents, giving them a hearty hug that I could have sworn creaked dust from the dried dirt on her father's jacket. "Mama, Papa, I want you to meet my Clan!"

Her parents, despite their rugged appearance, were really friendly and had a sort of kindness you knew was genuine.

At Group earlier that day, we found out that Dannie was leaving. She had been the Group's leader and crutch. Whenever there was something that needed to be done and no one wanted to do it, Dannie did it. She and I didn't have a lot in common, but I liked her and I trusted her.

Before, I never trusted any of my friends. They were people I used for things or people who entertained me. But now trust was the foundation of my friendships.

Inside, I felt like a puppy watching my sister being adopted and having to stay behind at the loud, dirty pet store.

That night, I lay in bed and thought of Matt, just like every other night. I wondered how he would be when I got back, or whether he would be there at all. *Is he thinking about me like I'm thinking about him? Was he still mad about the hickey, or did he believe it was the kitten?* My questions wouldn't be answered for months. Or even years, for all I knew.

TIME: 5:53 pm   **PATIENT NAME: Abigail Vona**

Group Treatment note: Patient checked into Group Treatment as feeling "content and relieved." Patient called time to talk about her ex-boyfriend and stated, "I was gamey with him but I ended up feeling close and I wanted to take care of him but I know I need to let him go." Patient seemed to give good feedback to her peers.

- Dr. K. Wisely

Day 141

The next morning after showers, I watched Rochelle flipping her hair. My eyes fixed on strange-looking blotches on her neck. They didn't look like birthmarks or scars. I had noticed the strange rash before but dismissed it. But it had grown since I had last seen Rochelle at the shower. It could be contagious, I thought. Medical issues were taken very seriously and were strictly confidential at The Village. And everything was very hidden. Even when you asked for a tampax it was something top secret. We did not even know who was having her period.

I felt obliged to point out the rash to Rochelle — she would never see it without a mirror.

Rochelle got very concerned and upset.

Miss Strickler called for two nurses who came all the way out to the cabin. I knew that Miss Strickler wouldn't have given it a second thought if I had a rash on my neck. But there was a big difference between my history and Rochelle's. I was a virgin who never saw much of the streets, Rochelle was a prostitute from Los Angeles with the nickname "Diamond." I worried that Rochelle's rash might be something she picked up from one of her johns or even her pimp, Joaquin.

TIME: 8:13 am   **PATIENT NAME: Abigail Vona**

Milieu Treatment note: Abigail seemed to interact with peers on a minimal level. Her hygiene appeared unkempt and disheveled. Three to four dark red sores were discovered by staff on the center of her back during showers.

- B. Rossly

Day 142

"Well Abby, we are really proud about how you are doing," said Miss Fawn. Then she hammered into my head how I needed to be polite and keep the session with my stepmom superficial. And the most important thing was not bring up or even think of my mom.

Miss Fawn was a funny woman and when issues of importance came up, she seemed to rehearse what she would say, making her sound like a bad reporter. If she hadn't just mentioned stepmom stuff then I would probably have appreciated the humor in her behavior.

"Does this mean that I'll have therapy with my mom too?" I asked.

Miss Fawn sat up. "We will have therapy with your mom in the future but you need to focus on therapy with your dad because you'll be living with him, and Judy is a big part of his life." Miss Fawn said, looking as nervous as I felt. I wondered if she was fresh out of college and this was her first therapy job. But I knew she wouldn't tell me if I asked. Staff never told you anything about their home life or past. "Anything you want to get off your chest before therapy, Abby?"

I shook my head. Why am I doing this? I had agreed to having therapy with the woman I hated more than any other person. But I clearly had no choice.

"Okay, we'll call." Miss Fawn messed up a few times before dialing the number. "Tired," she said, making a fake yawn. It came across to me as being more jumpy than tired. But I chose to ignore it. I wondered how my stepmom would act. She was an expert at pissing me off until I flipped out and had a temper tantrum. I didn't want to do that today.

Every time the phone rang I took a breath of air. I had trouble getting enough oxygen into my lungs. Finally, Judy answered, "Hello." Her voice was exactly how I remembered it. A voice I hated.

"Hi, this is Miss Fawn, and I have Abby on the phone, too."

I had a sudden urge to hang up the phone but forced myself to say, "Hi Judy, how are you?"

"Oh Abby, I'm glad to hear from you. It seems forever since I've heard your voice. Boy, do you sound different," she said all happy.

I didn't think her cheerfulness was honest at all. She wasn't really glad to talk to me. "Boy, do you sound different." With five words, she was making fun of the fact that I had told my dad I had changed.

It took a lot of effort for me to say anything.

If Miss Fawn hadn't been there it would have ended that moment. "Yeah, it's been a long time. Boy, you sound the same as the last time I spoke to you."

An awkward few seconds went by.

"Well your dad tells me you are really doing well. I'm proud."

"Proud," I thought. She couldn't be proud. Only a person who cared for you had the right to be proud. And she doesn't care.

"I've been working hard and doing all right," I added.

"That's good, good."

Another awkward silence.

"How's the weather down in Tennessee? I've never been down there. I imagine it's nicer than here."

It went downhill from there. Our conversation ended up becoming not only meaningless, but even more awkward. But I was surprised at how nice she turned out to be and I couldn't help but wonder about the reason behind it. When therapy was over. I felt as if I had conquered something. I had conquered Judy. I showed her.

TIME: 3:48 pm   **PATIENT NAME: Abigail Vona**

Group Treatment note: Patient stated feeling "okay." Patient stated, "I used people. I was afraid to tell them I liked them. I'd tell myself I liked them for their car or money. When we stopped being friends, I'd feel bad for even liking them. I'm scared to tell someone that I like them or have fun with them." Patient seemed attentive and offered feedback.

- Dr. K. Wisely

Chapter 5

VOID

Day 145

This was the first Thanksgiving that I wouldn't be home in my entire life. I had always taken spending the holidays with my family for granted. And most of the time they sucked. But after a while, you kind of felt really good being with your family, like you've just done a good deed or something. I wondered what they were doing now, or if they were even thinking of me, asking where I was.

Staff told us we would do something special for the holiday. But it was the same time goals and Consequence as every day, and breakfast was nothing special either. I was starting to think that Staff had lied but then the Frog Clan came into the cafeteria with two men carrying a large TV and VCR.

We were allowed to look at the Frog Clan. It was the first time I saw Amy and Katherine since they were on STU. Amy looked happy, Katherine looked okay too. They tried to smile with a bunch of other freaky girls I didn't know.

Most of the girls in the Frog Clan were anorexics and bulimics and many of them were paying, as opposed to The Coyote Clan, which was mostly girls with anger, drug, prostitution, and stealing problems. Plus, most of Coyote came from the court and the state.

"Are you ready for one of the best Thanksgivings ever?"

yelled one of the Frog Staff. While we threw away our things from breakfast, Miss Rossly and the Frog Staff made trips in and out, bringing in colored paper, glitter, and lots of old movie videos.

Four hours later, I had to admit that the woman was right. As tacky as it sounds, that was the funnest day of my life. Only under severe agony can you really appreciate good things. Those movies were the best movies I ever watched — *E.T.*, *Footloose*, and *The Lion King*. It wasn't that they were my favorites, but because I hadn't watched a movie in what seemed forever, I was beyond entertained.

TIME: 7:39 am   **PATIENT NAME: Abigail Vona**

Individual Psychotherapy note: During this session Abigail discussed a new treatment intervention, one in which her dazed demeanor is controlled. She described feeling angry. Abigail described her tendency of retreating into her thoughts as a way to deal with feelings. She described that her thought process entails her creating a story relevant to the particular feeling or reflecting on a story/movie with a relevant feeling. Abigail stated that she has been coping in this way all her life. We discussed that this is no longer adaptive and she needs to develop more appropriate means to expressing her feelings.

- Dr. K. Wisely

Day 153

"No, bitch, I'm not doing them," Candace growled, giving Miss Rossly one of her famous I-worship-the-devil-and-am-cursing-you-to-hell looks. We were at the garden site and Candace did not want to shovel.

"You know nothing," said Candace, trying to stare down Miss

Rossly. "I hope you die a terrible death. I hope you go to hell! And you will because I am going to put you there."

Candace thought she was an evil witch putting a curse on someone, but it wasn't working because Candace wasn't a demon. She was just a kid who hated the world, and herself. Actually, she was a waste of food and oxygen.

"Candace, if you don't get up now and do your push-ups, I'll have to force you to do them and you don't want that." Miss Grout's words blasted through my ears. She was a mean-looking woman but as kind as they come. This was the first time I saw her genuinely angry and it wasn't pretty.

"Miss Grout, shut up. You're just mad 'cause God made you the ugliest, stupidest woman. You wouldn't be here with us unless you had no life and you were stupid!"

The words made me want to get up and smack Candace. I loved Miss Grout and knew she was hurt. But she didn't show it. She just went over to assist Candace with her push-ups. Candace began to fight, struggling against her. "Mary, blow the horn!" Miss Grout said, keeping her cool.

Twelve Staff came running out of nowhere, including Miss Strickler. I wondered if in the application to work there, they asked if you're a good runner.

"Miss Grout, I hope you die from cancer. I hope you do, too, Miss Strickler." There was a pause. Suddenly there was blood all over Miss Grout's face and jacket.

"Oh my God, blood, help me get it off!" she shrieked.

Miss Grout abandoned her job of holding Candace's left arm down and instead frantically wiped her face with a clean part of the sleeve of her jacket. Meanwhile, Candace's arm was pumping defiantly while she yelled.

"Ahh, go on you fuckin' bitch, whine. I hope you fucking die!"

Miss Grout got her composure back. She went back to holding down Candace's arm.

I had never witnessed one of Candace's restraints, but Ally had told me about them. "Her restraints are outrageous. She shouts 'You'll die in a car crash' or 'I just gave you AIDS.' If she had lived a hundred years ago, they would have hung her with the rest of the witches."

This time Candace had cut open her mouth with her teeth so she could spit tons of blood at Miss Grout.

All of a sudden I thought about all the fucked up things I did, even though I wasn't nearly as bad. Maybe Candace and I do crazy things for similar reasons. Candace probably spits blood for attention. Maybe that's why I stole. But it wasn't. I stole to fill myself up. *I can't explain it and I don't know if it makes sense but it's like I have a hole and am looking for something to fill it. People can't fill this hole. They're too unpredictable and when they disappoint me the hole just grows. Stealing makes up for that.*

TIME: 11:04 pm   **PATIENT NAME: Abigail Vona**

Milieu Treatment note: Patient's affect appeared quiet and sneaky throughout the day. She required a high level of staff directives to follow unit guidelines. She seemed to consistently approach staff to attempt to manipulate unit guidelines.

- N. Strickler

Day 177

"It's the AA lady, Abby," said Miss Rossly, looking out the window.

There was a knock on our cabin door and a large, plump

woman in colorful southwestern garb walked in.

"Hi y'all, here to pick up Abby."

She wore a red patterned Christmas scarf with yellow bells that matched her red spandex pants. Her huge coat covered most of her body, and her hair, which was pulled back in a bun, had frizzy pieces poking out on all sides. I introduced myself and she gave me a warm smile.

"Hi. My name is Abby. Nice to meet you."

"I'm Miss Dunkler, nice to meet you, Abby. Oh, you're so polite."

I didn't think much of my politeness. It was a southern thing so I just did it too. I actually liked it, and the difference from before was huge.

We drove to the STU building and found an empty office. The Village brought in an AA member for Step Five, which is basically a confession minus the priest. I wondered if Staff thought I had some secret past that I was hiding, and when I confessed to the AA person then they would trap me.

It felt weird talking to a stranger but she was such a jolly woman. She was like a Mrs. Santa Claus who lived in the South. Miss Dunkler told me about her alcoholism, having to give up her baby for adoption and trying to commit suicide. It was hard to believe.

"I owe my life to AA," she said with so much passion as we sat eating sandwiches. "Now, Abby, don't be afraid to tell me what you want. It's only between you and me, confidential always." She zipped her lip up and I knew she meant what she said.

I told her about everything I did and everything I stole. She asked me why I did these things. I said, "I steal to make people angry and because I want things."

Miss Dunkler looked unsatisfied with my reason.

"There must be a stronger motivation besides pissing off your father and greed. I know when I was in your shoes, I said I drank because I liked to drink but my reason behind drinking was my constant desire to fill a void inside me. There is a loneliness that I feel and have felt since I can remember and I tried to fill it up with alcohol but instead it consumed me."

I knew the void Miss Dunkler described as loneliness. I also felt it, but unlike normal loneliness, meaning you only feel lonely when there's no one with you, this loneliness is so deep that it hurts even when you're surrounded by friends. I wondered why some people felt this way. Did my stealing fill the empty space?

I *was* lonely, but I didn't know why, or what from. Maybe from my mom and dad splitting up, or my mom and dad not paying enough attention to me as a kid. They were fighting throughout the end of the marriage. I was a mistake. My dad hated my mom so much, that he fucked another woman even before I was born. As I grew up, things didn't get any better.

I told Miss Dunkler about this and she knew what I meant. I felt relieved.

TIME: 6:12 pm   PATIENT NAME: Abigail Vona

Individual Psychotherapy note: Abigail was quite angry and frustrated with her older brother. Abigail was very focused on making a pamphlet of the "12 Steps" as a gift for her brother. Session was focused on exploring the underlying reason for her gift. Abigail explained that she wanted to convey to her brother that she cares for him and does not want him to continue hurting himself.

- Dr. K. Wisely

Chapter 6

BEDLAM

Day 180

The first week of Shut Down was a blur of restraints and tears. We did nothing besides eat, sit on our beds, and sleep. Every other day, they took us in pairs of two to the bathhouse to take a shower. The days we didn't shower our hygiene consisted of patting our faces with a washcloth dampened by the Gott water, and brushing our teeth and spitting the paste into a bucket. For some reason, Shut Down seemed a billion times worse than being on STU, even though it was basically the same thing.

Candace was getting more violent in her resistance to being restrained. A couple of days before, she was able to push Miss Rossly onto her butt. Staff then took her to the ground, stopping her from running away.

I looked out at the light snowfall. Staff let me work on my Steps when things were quiet. I had to write down all the stuff I wanted to give up in my life. I was waiting to burn it in the fire to confirm it. Miss Dunkler had recommended burning Step Six paper in a fire, combining the step with an old Indian ritual. Giving things up was going to be fucking well easier said than done. I was confident I would never smoke, but lying, stealing, and Matt were three things I worried about.

TIME: 5:13 pm   **PATIENT NAME:** Abigail Vona

Group Treatment note: Patient checked in feeling emotionally scattered, depressed and sad. Patient stated "I feel I'm in a huge cloud of chaos. I'm not seeing things clearly. I feel I'm focusing on problems too much. It's confusing. I think clearly, but fall apart over and over. I think about my life; I screw up, I must do this, I got to do this, or do less, maybe I'm crazy, maybe I need to focus more or I do too much. I'm so tired. I've been doing it a long time. I feel I can't think rationally but I know I can. It's happening a lot and I don't know what to do." Patient seemed scattered and fearful throughout disclosures.

                                        - Dr. K. Wisely

Day 184

Christmas morning we were woken up by Miss Strickler dressed from head to toe in bright red and a white trimmed Santa hat.

"Ho, ho, ho . . . I let you sleep one hour later and you better have enjoyed it."

She then handed out NA books to all of us, as we climbed out of our beds.

This was a welcome change. The day before, Mary had left for good. The whole group was sad to see her go.

Candace sat on her bed with her eyes half-closed, her fingers pressed against her thumbs Indian-style as if becoming possessed. She then got up off her bed and told us all how she made love to Satan himself and would carry the Antichrist. She was restrained in the middle of describing her sex life with the devil. I saw this coming, because I knew her patterns. When a peer left, Candace would get upset. She couldn't handle it and would flip out.

After Candace calmed down, Shut Down rules were briefly

lifted. Sitting in a Group to eat meant conversation out of Group Therapy and I was dying to talk to anyone. We sat in a circle on the floor having senseless conversations. Then we played board games and got mail, which had been kept from us until now.

I received two cards from my dad and stepmother and six from my Mom. I took a breath and opened my stepmother's letter.

Hi, Abby. I was told about the hard times you are going through and I'm truly sorry.

I know that you and I never really hit it off and I'm truly sorry we didn't. I think you're a great person and hope next Christmas will make up for all the Christmases we never had.

Love,

Judy

I put down the letter, not believing a word. *Who does she think she is, my mother?* Steaming with anger, sitting on the floor and trying to hold back from crying, I watched all the excited faces open their Christmas cards. I hated myself for being jealous of their happiness but instead found myself wishing to go back to my bed.

"Abby, you're not in the Christmas spirit at all." I looked up and saw Miss Strickler with her Santa Claus hat. "You need to call a Group."

I read the letter out loud and expressed my thoughts of Judy deceiving me. Candace wasn't even paying attention, she was reading her letters. I decided to involve just Ally and Rochelle and pretend the rest didn't exist. Ally had a God-given wisdom about her that probably came from coping with the fucked-up life she had. And Rochelle, with her unique past, would make a good Oprah-type interviewer. They had compassion and I trusted them.

"I wonder if I'm just paranoid about my stepmother because I don't want her to be the mother I never had," I expressed.

"I think the letter is appropriate, and she is making an effort to connect with you," Ally said, bringing up the fact that I never really accepted Judy, that maybe it was me.

When Ally told me, I actually listened.

TIME: 3:43 pm   **PATIENT NAME: Abigail Vona**

Group Treatment note: Patient described her relationship with her stepmother, and seemed to frequently contradict herself. Patient alternately explained that she and her stepmother "did not talk," "went to Disney on Ice together," and "sometimes had a positive relationship." Patient seemed to argue with staff input about these contradictions, and appeared to become flustered at this time.

- Dr. K. Wisely

Day 190

One Monday morning, Miss Strickler came into the cabin with a black-haired girl who looked grim. It was Katherine.

When we started Group she went first. "Hi, I'm Katherine," she said with no feeling, just like she sounded on STU. "I got kicked out of the Frog Clan," she said, swinging her foot like a two-year-old. "I regressed." Her foot halted mid-swing and she suddenly got very angry. "I was doing good and then it happened, I gave up. It got too hard. One of my problems is that I think in black and white — meaning I see all good, or all bad, not seeing the big picture and there is no in-between." She went back to swinging her foot again, as though it helped jog along the memory. "When I got restrained, everything was lost, and I haven't been able to get it back again.

"I know the cutting is a problem but I do it because I don't feel anything when I cut, except for the cut itself."

I suddenly had a realization, remembering the incident on STU with Miss Curran when I got the rope burn and how ice numbed it. How I would rather feel the cold than the throbbing pain. I told Katherine this and after explaining my ice theory, and relating it to her cutting, her eyes lit up.

"Y'all," she said, "when I cut, it sort of numbs my insides. Like Abby's ice, cutting numbs my pain and lets me concentrate on only one thing, the cut. My cutting may be bad, but it makes me hurt less." Her issue became clear to me and now I understood something I never thought I would.

TIME: 6:02 am   **PATIENT NAME: Abigail Vona**

Milieu Treatment note: Patient remains on Shut Down with her peer group due to negative, unsafe, disrespectful, and aggressive behaviors.

- N. Strickler

Day 196

I had come to the conclusion that we would never get off Shut Down. In the last week, Candace had been restrained five times, screaming once at Miss Stricker, "I'm going to kill you!"

Candace took all her anger out on Miss Strickler. Some of what Candace said was true: that Miss Strickler was a greedy person, and that she liked to eat her candy bars and junk cereal right in front of us but never offered any. Candace called her a "fat, greedy dyke-bitch," which was true, except I didn't think Miss Strickler was a lesbian. I didn't think she was anything.

We sat on our beds all day. Rochelle made fish lips, obviously as bored as me. I closed my eyes and tried to remember every building I was ever in during my entire life.

I mentally walked through homes, schools, theaters, even a funeral parlor. It's amazing how good your memory is when you're bored out of your mind. I got homesick when I went through my own house and my old school. I decided to stop after picturing my school, which seemed to scorch my brain. I actually missed it. Why does everything good have to die or go away? I started to cry, partly because of not being in a normal school and the other part from pure unhappiness. I hated Shut Down.

That evening, Candace's breathing became loud and intense. She sounded like a rabid wolf, ready to attack. Something was bottled up inside her. It always was.

"Stop breathing like that," Miss Strickler ordered.

"This is how I breathe, you got a fuckin' problem?"

Candace started to breathe louder and louder, making me feel as if I walked in on an exorcism. Miss Strickler put her magazine down and got up out of her chair. Uh oh.

"Stop breathing like that or I'll . . ."

"Or you'll what?" Candace straightened up. "You're going to come over here and stop me from breathing?"

Candace had a point. Miss Strickler couldn't do anything, and in my opinion should have ignored Candace altogether. Miss Strickler was stubborn though.

"Do twenty push-ups for being rude," Miss Strickler said.

Candace stopped her breathing and laughed, "Fuck you, why don't you come over here and make me?"

Miss Strickler got heated and angry. "Miss Rossly, please help me escort Candace."

When two Staff moved toward a patient for an escort or a restraint, they worked as a team. They always did it together. And there was a reason.

Pissed off, Miss Strickler walked way in front of Miss Rossly. So, Candace got up and moved toward Miss Strickler. For a moment, they were face to face — Miss Strickler and crazy Candace.

"You fuckin' bitch!" Candace cried out like an Indian warrior, if Indian warriors said things like that, "I'm gonna fucking tear you apart!" Miss Strickler had this look of fear in that split second, a look which I never expected to see. She knew something bad was about to happen. Candace took full advantage of there being only one Staff in front of her. She punched Miss Strickler hard in the face and then in the head with all the crazy power she had. Miss Strickler fell in a heap down on the ground. It was like a boxing match when all of a sudden one guy hits the other and the other just falls to the ground like he's dead.

Candace continued to pound and kick Miss Strickler. Miss Rossly jumped on Candace, trying to save her friend. Blood gushed from Miss Strickler's nose, and her arm dangled at a weird angle. She tried to stand up and was kicked in the face again by Candace, and this time she was knocked unconscious.

"Rochelle, ring the air horn!" Miss Rossly yelled in total desperation. Rochelle was frozen and just sat on her bed, jaw open. She couldn't move. All of us just stared. I wanted to help with restraining Candace but we were not allowed to help, ever. It was a very strict rule, even if Staff was getting the shit kicked out of them.

Candace was medium size but very strong and at this point, possessed. She threw Miss Rossly off her back and grabbed the air horn herself, ripping off the top and breaking it apart, and throwing it on separate sides of the cabin. The unthinkable had happened, a kid was now in control!

"All of you help me out!" Candace screamed. But we sat on our beds, still. Months before, maybe I would have helped but not now. I was scared and angry but I couldn't do anything. And Rochelle just sat there in fear. Miss Rossly flung herself on Candace, trying to take her to the ground.

"Abby, run to the cafeteria and get Staff. "

At first I couldn't believe my ears, I wasn't allowed to do that.

"*Now,* Abby!" Miss Rossly screamed at me as Candace pulled Miss Rossly's red hair out.

I jumped off my bed and ran for the door. I ran as fast as I could in the dark, not believing my ultimate freedom. It was like a dream, running at night alone in the dark. It felt so good.

When I got to the cafeteria, I realized how strange it would be for Staff to see me, a patient telling them about the out-of-control restraint. I stood in front of the closed door to the cafeteria. Would they restrain me for walking on my own?

I took a deep breath and opened the door. Three male Staff sat at an open table, playing cards. They looked up at me, disbelieving. I looked at them, afraid of what to say. Two of the three men were young. One had a heavy build. The other was shorter and had blond hair that didn't coincide with his huge tattoos. The third guy was old and wore his long hair in a ponytail. He had a big gut. The young ones were handsome. I wasn't supposed to even look at the male patients or Staff but sometimes I caught a glimpse of these three men. This all but made up for the times I couldn't look.

They started to get up from their chairs, slowly, ready to chase me down and restrain me if I was running astray from my Group. The oldest man had a bewildered expression. "Where's your Group?" he asked just as the others moved in to escort me. I snapped out of it. "My Group, they're, they're, they need your help . . . Candace . . ." I didn't even finish my sentence and they understood. All Staff knew about Candace.

"Go to the Coyote Cabin, you two, Now! I'll babysit this Coyote," said the old man.

The two young men ran off, leaving me with the old man.

"Hi, my name's Austin," he said, putting out his hand for me to shake. I put out mine.

"I'm Abby."

The old man had an odd manner about him. He was one of those people you don't trust until they talk and then something about their gestures and mellow tone of voice relaxes you. People like that are like horse whisperers, but for delinquent kids, and they are hard to come by. I knew I could talk to him.

"You like cards?" He pointed to the table.

After two months of Shut Down and isolation, playing poker with a strange old man at nine o'clock at night was great. We talked for three hours about what happened. I told him everything about my life. Then he told me about the boys' Cabins, the differences in rules and past stories. He told me about an ex-patient who killed his father, and when he was at The Village he told Austin about his father torturing him.

"Everything happens for a reason," Austin said. "Sometimes it's not for a good, fair, or just reason, but it's always a reaction to a past event or a chemical imbalance in the head."

Austin told me the boys called their Staff by their first names and the girls program should do the same. He told me all my Staff's first names. Strickler-Nancy, Rossly-Megan, Grout-Tiffany. Then he said in a chuckle, "One day call them by their first names. It would be funny." I pictured me getting a thousand pyramid tens for calling Miss Strickler "Nancy" and decided not to do what Austin suggested.

Although I had lots of fun playing poker and listening to Austin, I was very worried about what was happening at the cabin. I was still jittery. I pictured Candace decapitating Miss Strickler and then Miss Rossly with a maul as the Group lay on their beds like corpses. I hoped the two young Staff got there in time.

It wasn't until midnight that one of the men returned.

"How'd it go?" asked Austin.

When the man got closer to us, I noticed he had blood on his shirt. "Miss Rossly's all right," he said in a thick southern accent. "Miss Strickler's gone to the hospital." The man wiped his head with a clean part of his sleeve. "It was pretty bad," he shook his head at Austin, "but she'll be okay."

"The girl, Candace, I believe?" He looked at me and I nodded. "Well, she ran when she saw us coming. We caught up with her way out in the woods. She's in police custody, they got her tranquilized in an ambulance."

I couldn't believe Miss Strickler was hurt. I worried about her. As much as I didn't get along with her she was growing on me. She was a big part of my life.

"Miss Rossly's up there now. Paul's filling in for Nancy."

"What will happen to Candace?" I asked because I didn't think there was therapy out here that would fix her. Maybe a lobotomy, but the Staff would never do that, even with this.

"Well," he said, surprisingly sympathetic, "Candace will go to STU where she'll be provided for."

I didn't know what that meant, "She'll be provided for." It sounded like code for something else. They had a lot words that meant something else here like "escort," "process," and "Consequence." For all I knew, "provided for" meant "lobotomized." Which, by the way, would have been fine with me.

TIME: 4:46 am   **PATIENT NAME: Abigail Vona**

Milieu Treatment note: Patient appears to sleep soundly.

                                             - Night Staff

Day 197

I sat in Miss Fawn's office with my ear pressed against the phone, waiting for them to answer the ringing. I was not prepared to face them both.

My dad picked up the phone. "Hey, Abby." The sound from the phone told me he was on the speaker.

"Hi," I answered.

"I heard you're off Shut Down," my stepmother said, letting me know she was in the room.

"Yeah, we're doing well as a Group." It was true, without Candace we were getting along really well and working as a team. Even Katherine.

"I heard about you being the little hero," my dad said, with an unfamiliar pride in his voice.

"Yup."

"Why don't you talk about your Step work?" Miss Fawn suggested, picking up on the fact the conversation was going to crash in about ten seconds.

So, I tried to be honest. I told Judy how I was wrong to steal her things, vandalize her clothes and swear at her. She was cool about my apology and said she was sorry for losing her temper and trying to replace my mother. I began to understand and respect her in a way. The therapy was actually working and both our true colors came out. She ended up crying about how she wanted things to be perfect and always wanted a relationship with me but was overwhelmed. That made me cry too.

It was strange not having an enemy anymore. I felt empty in a good way and wondered what I would do with all of the space, like a burden was lifted out of my soul.

Group Treatment note: Patient stated, "Before, I didn't really appreciate my father, I thought he was an idiot and didn't know what he was talking about. I feel like I need help from my father, I feel better when supported by my father and I am trying to build a relationship with him." Patient stated, "Me and my mom are really close and similar, if I grow up it won't be the same. In a way I would lose my mom and our old relationship."

- Dr. K. Wisely

Chapter 7

PICNIC

Day 209

When Miss Strickler opened the door, we yelled, "Surprise!" She looked around at the "Welcome Back" balloons, cards, and banners filling up the cabin and smiled, "Thanks y'all, this is great."

But Miss Strickler didn't look excited, more like she was forcing herself to smile and get through it. She had a thick, bright pink cast on her right arm and a slightly bruised cheek. It had been over two weeks since Candace's uproar.

Miss Strickler didn't carry herself with as much strength and authority, and she looked slightly uncomfortable. I knew she prided herself on being thorough and strict and although the fact of her failure wasn't brought up, she seemed embarrassed by her mistakes, which had landed her in the hospital. She was definitely more human now and I knew she was embarrassed and dreaded facing us. A part of me admired her for having the courage to come back.

"I would like to apologize to you all," she said, just as we showered her with handmade confetti. "I'm sorry that you had to see me lose my temper, and though I'm not excusing Candace's behavior, I was also at fault."

Miss Strickler had all of us listening in awe. She had never admitted her wrongs before, and now this made me respect her even more. It was one thing to be a strong person, but it took a true leader to admit her faults, and that made me listen.

Miss Strickler and the Staff used to be my enemies; now they felt more like my allies.

TIME: 8:32 pm   **PATIENT NAME: Abigail Vona**

Milieu Treatment note: Abigail seemed to be in a fair humor throughout day. She left to speak to her mother via the phone. She seemed very upset when she returned to the group. She expressed that she and her mother talked about her brother. This conversation seemed to make Abigail cry.

- N. Strickler

Day 295

I was carrying logs at the wood-chopping site when Miss Strickler approached me.

"Abby, you know Easter is the day after tomorrow."

I shook my head. How could I know?

Miss Strickler took a few steps closer to bridge the gap between us, then in a whisper she said, "Your dad and stepmother, well, they asked special permission to see you on Easter."

I caught my breath. I couldn't believe it.

"We granted them permission, and you'll be able to take them and your brother on campus for a picnic from noon to five."

I had trouble both grasping this and breathing at the same time. I had to take in three deep breaths to calm my nerves. I hadn't seen my dad and brother for almost a year now, and my stepmother was absent from my life for a lot longer than that. Everything would have been fine if my brother hadn't been coming too. I had bad images of him doing everything from trying to pick up Rochelle, to pulling out a joint, or just acting like the degenerate ass that he is.

That afternoon at Group, I blabbed about how excited I was. It also made me think of the reality that someday I would have to leave this place. How would I cope? *What if my stepmom picks a fight? What if I become a total bitch again? What if my father ignores me?* I was glad to have a day to prepare myself.

I wrote "action plans" for the next day — what I should do when one thing or another happened: if I disobeyed the rules, I would run and tell my dad. If my brother acted up, I would ignore him. My stepmom worried me. Miss Rossly suggested the most effective and ridiculous thing — I act out the "what if" my stepmother flips out. Rochelle pretended to be Judy, putting on a Boston accent. She reminded me of the sitcom *The Nanny*, saying, "Abby, I know you've worked hard to ruin you father's life and my life, but . . ." or "Gee, I guess this place didn't make you any smarter, did it?" or "Abby, we found a nice boarding school for you, in Australia!" and trying to make me mad. She did manage to ruffle my feathers, but I kept my cool.

TIME: 7:08 pm   **PATIENT NAME: Abigail Vona**

Group Treatment note: Patient checked into this session feeling emotionally "excited and anxious." She called time to talk about her upcoming visit from her brother. She became overwhelmed when she began speaking about him saying, "Once he backed me up in the corner of the car . . . and said that Dad would kill me if I got out of the car while he wasn't there." She seemed very nervous but remained focused.

                                        - Dr. K. Wisely

Day 296

At 11:55, I stood waiting for them to arrive, breathing deeply and wishing I could have brought Ally and Rochelle with me. When I saw my family, I felt giddy, happy, like an excited little girl. Looking at them in the distance, they seemed so unreal. Everything from my past had been taken away. It was almost like all of us were new people meeting for the first time. Now they were here, in my new life, to tell me about the home I would be returning to and the other life I would someday have to live.

When they got closer, my dad and stepmother yelled, "Hi, Abby." And in my excitement, I cast away the hopeless, jealous feelings I had been having.

Our reunion was awkward. The only time I had ever really gotten along with them was over the phone. My stepmom's greeting reminded me of how you would meet a penpal. But I didn't mind and expected nothing more. They both carried large brown bags with sandwiches and soda inside.

"You ready for a picnic?" my dad said, excited to see the Tennessee landscape. He was a nature buff. My brother said "hi" under his breath and watched suspiciously as the Coyote Clan walked away.

My stepmom held up a sandwich, "I know how much you like tuna." Then I saw something I never bothered to see before. Ally was right. My stepmother was really making an effort to please me, she really did try. I was the one who rejected *her*.

We walked down to the ropes course to have a picnic by the river. When one of the boys' clans walked by, my brother watched them closely. He knew that he should have been here too. "This place is crazy. What do they do, brainwash you? They won't even look at us." I had a debate in my head if I should even answer this

— my anger and resentment got the best of me.

"We're not allowed to look at other clans. We're supposed to be focusing on our own treatment." My brother scrunched up his face as if to tell me I was brainwashed too. I was glad that my stepmom butted in, "So Abby, how do you like your clan?"

We set up our picnic at the ropes site and watched the birds build their nests on the cliff ledges. We talked about the future, a bittersweet subject because I really liked The Village now. My stepmom asked where I wanted to go to school next fall, and I was glad she gave me the option, not demanding anything of me. We were excited. My brother didn't say much during any of the conversation.

As we finished eating, my brother pulled out a cigarette and lit it with the Gucci lighter he stole from me. I was tempted to ask him to give it back, but then realized that I didn't really want it anymore.

"You're not supposed to smoke on the property," my father said, trying to act calm.

"This place is a fuckin' freakshow and I don't give a fuck what the rules are, I don't go to school here."

My dad and stepmom just sat there munching on chips. For some reason I was angrier that he called this place a school than the fact that he called me a freak. Why didn't my father put him in STU like he did to me?

But I said, "You're the one who has an addiction, you're the one who should be here, your problems . . ."

"Fuck you," he said with a sneer and walked away.

Please Dad, put him in STU. I could have Staff here in two minutes.

My dad followed my brother saying, "Ted, please calm down." He still pushed my father around. It was all the same. I started to cry. My dad had not seen me for a year and here he was talking to my brother.

I didn't want to cry. I was the grown-up and they were the children now. I was so filled with hatred and sadness. I hated that my stepmom was there to see me like this and I put my head down trying to hide myself. She came over and put her arms around me. We stayed like that until Ted and my dad came back.

After that, no one really talked. I expected Ted to apologize, then realized that was not him. People here did that. People here were better. *That's not what it's like in the real world.*

It wasn't long before I was back with my Group, watching my dad and stepmom walk away. I felt split between by my Group and my family. No, I didn't, I liked my Group more.

TIME: 2:00 pm   **PATIENT NAME: Abigail Vona**

Individual Psychotherapy note: Abigail processed her recent 2-day visits with her father and older brother. As she processed, she appeared quite upset. She experienced tremendous difficulty when she attempted to put her feelings into words. It appeared that her thoughts became somewhat disorganized and her words mumbled. She attempted to defend against these feelings by quietly dismissing her impressions or rationalizing them. When this defense was noted to her she began to describe feelings of anger and disappointment with her brother. She also described feelings of loss, for her old self and her old relationship with her brother.

- Dr. K. Wisely

Chapter 8

A PRAYER FOR ROCHELLE

Day 297

Candace came back.

She made a brief apology to the Group, Miss Strickler, and Miss Rossly and she took a bunk. The Group was upset and did not want her there. And I bet Miss Strickler and Miss Rossly felt the same. Candace had good qualities, but she was also scary and dangerous. We had been off Shut Down since she left. But with her in the cabin, it was only a matter of days until we went back on.

It was a strange situation. Miss Strickler still had her cast. Candace had been the one who put her in the hospital and might have killed her. But there was nothing that Miss Strickler could do because Candace was a "state" kid. Some bureaucrat for the state of Tennessee just told The Village, "Tough, she has to stay there because we don't have anywhere else to put her." I heard Staff complain about this, but there was nothing they could do. If you're a state kid, you probably have to murder someone before they take you out.

The other problem was that sometimes girls acted up because they wanted to stay at The Village. At first I would never have understood this, but now I did. Many girls here had been abandoned or had abandonment issues, including me. Kids like Candace acted up to stay *in*.

Candace spent therapy talking about how things were going really well with her grandmother and how they were going to live together.

Ally listened to Candace with a look of disgust. "Why'd you put your grandma through so much hell if you love her so much?"

Candace, obviously due to her selfishness or just wanting to piss Ally off said, "Well, families forgive each other if they really care."

It was too bad, because a real grandmother like Candace had would have given Ally a reason to like her life and make something of herself.

TIME: 5:28 pm   **PATIENT NAME: Abigail Vona**

Group Treatment note: Patient called time to discuss how she loves art. "I really like to do art. I got into other things before I came here, like clubbing and being with people to impress them. I didn't really like clubbing. Yeah, it's cool, to tell other people I went clubbing. I was focused on what guys thought of me. I let other things get in the way. I really like decorating the bedroom or making clothes. I feel good about my room and miss my room. I feel secure there."

- Dr. K. Wisely

Day 298

I had to make a list of people I hurt and be willing to make amends with them. I took Step Eight very seriously and was very thorough, writing down every person I had harmed even in the slightest bit. This was also a time-consuming Step, because there were lists and lists of people I had harmed.

After doing this Step, I made a commitment to myself to be careful not to add anyone new to the list. For instance, when I left a lantern at the cabin I would not only do my pyramid tens but I offered to hold the lantern for a month instead of a week because I didn't want to harm the Group. Or when I looked after Rochelle's boots but accidentally left them in the rain, I not only did one hundred push-ups but also let her use my dry boots. My charitable efforts didn't go unnoticed and Staff gave me more privileges, like taking the garbage out to the dumpster, carrying Staff bags or walking to get things Staff forgot. I was completely trusted, which was strange. I had always been the least trusted . . . here *and* on the outside. Staff said I was "care-taking," which turned out not to be as good as it sounded.

Because of my care-taking, I was now "on rest" from chores, meaning I was only allowed to do things that were fun but nothing that wasn't. This happened after I got in trouble for leaving Gott cups at the garden site and then offered to not only do my push-ups but be put on the Gott for a week, alone. This was a chore that everyone hated, even for a day, let alone a week. Candace looked ecstatic to have me take over the Gott, and a crooked smile spread across her face. She wasn't the only one who was smiling. Miss Strickler had a smile too, but the semi-amused one that I only saw on bad occasions.

"Abby . . . Abby . . . Abby . . . why are you care-taking for the Group?"

I opened my mouth to say, "Step Eight, ma'am'" but she went on talking, letting me know she wanted to make an example of me.

"You're giving too much to the Group and taking over others' responsibilities, not allowing them to learn. Now, I want you to not have any responsibilities. You have become the Group's slave. I'm afraid they need to run things on their own."

Actually, Miss Strickler was getting less and less unbearable to be around. I didn't feel like I was being watched by a temperamental guard-dog anymore. After Miss Strickler's verdict, I did nothing.

Having no responsibilities sounds nice but in reality it's much worse. When I had my jobs, I got them done on time and efficiently and it gave me something to focus on. But watching Candace do my jobs slowly and half-assed annoyed me and gave my Group more Consequences. I wanted my "vacation" to end.

TIME: 2:19 pm   **PATIENT NAME: Abigail Vona**

Milieu Treatment note: She was called upon several times for staring at male staff, knowing full well that she was doing wrong.

- N. Strickler

Day 299

Miss Strickler yelled at us saying, "If you act like chickens with your heads cut off, then we will have to cancel." That sure calmed us down. When we got into the white van and pulled out of The Village, I could have screamed with anticipation.

As we walked into the building, I held my head up with an inner pride I hadn't possessed before. I didn't feel better than everyone else, just happy for myself. I wore the same clothes, but this time it hardly fazed me. We walked into the auditorium and took our seats. But this time I felt no concern about how the crowd perceived me.

"Hi, I'm Andy and I'm an alcoholic."

"Hi, Andy," we answered back.

"We all know that wisdom doesn't always come with age and some youngsters can be the most wise. I'd like to introduce a boy who is only nineteen, but is just as much a part of AA, NA as any other recovering addict. Jason, will you come up on stage."

A tall young man made his way up. He wore faded ripped jeans and a tee shirt saying "Rock on MTV." His arms were covered with tattoos of marijuana leaves, naked fairies, and abstract patterns. He looked like a thief, druggie, and rapist but carried himself in a friendly and sophisticated way.

When he walked up to the podium and shook old Andy's hand, I got a closer look at him. He had dark eyes and hair and what appeared to be a knife scar on his cheek. He had probably been in some sort of gang. The thought of a Tennessee gang made me muffle a laugh. Jason took the mike from Andy and pulled out a piece of crumpled paper from his pocket. He looked nervous and read off the piece of paper.

"Hi, my name is Jason and I'm a recovering alcoholic and addict."

"Hi, Jason," the auditorium answered.

"I've been clean and sober for three years, and this program saved my life. I grew up in a broken home. I'm not blaming my pop, but he was a horrible example for a father, and it was a tragedy I looked up to him. He used to get drunk, beat my mom, beat me, and on occasion molested my sister."

The boy paused and choked. It was clearly hard for him to present his family's dirty laundry for all of us to see, but he looked determined to continue.

"A year after my sister committed suicide," he paused again to collect his thoughts, "I ran away. I lived in a coke-house and when it was torn down, I found another one.

"I was not only on coke but sold it. Once I even sold it to some eleven-year-olds, telling them it was good to try. I had so much guilt and sorrow, I feared I would either die or go slowly insane. I fed on drugs to hopefully make my problems disappear. But all it did was bring me more problems, and make me more ashamed of who I was. When I was sixteen, three years ago, I was finally arrested for possession of a gun and enough coke to put me behind bars for a very long time."

Jason seemed to gain confidence. As he went on with his story, he was able to put the piece of paper in his pocket.

"Every day, I thank God I was under age. I think jail is a place to learn more about the drug trade and trafficking, not to find a new life. Instead of jail, I went to a place that some people say is more intense than jail. I went to a facility, a boot camp for juveniles like myself, to learn to work the Steps and discuss our problems."

I couldn't believe my ears. He was at a place like The Village. I wondered how many places like The Village existed. I looked around at my Group. All of them looked just as curious as I did about the boy's past.

"At this place, I dug deep into my past and my issues, the ones that I had tried to cover up by taking drugs. I told my Staff. . ."

He talked like he went to The Village!

"I told them about my dad molesting my older sister, and then I testified in court. I not only put my dad behind bars, but may have saved my younger sister's life. The Steps became my guide to live life responsibly and have fun, enjoying things I had forgotten how to enjoy. Now I'm happy. That's my story. Thanks for letting me share."

We all stood up. I clapped until my hands hurt. Rochelle was happy — crying with a glow of hope and pride. His speech hit home for all of us. He was one of us.

TIME: 11:11 pm   **PATIENT NAME: Abigail Vona**

Group Treatment note: Patient expressed feeling nervous . . . Abigail stated, "I am afraid that if I quit zoning out I will lose part of my creativity and part of myself."

- Dr. K. Wisely

Day 302

"Now, Abby," Miss Fawn dialed nervously, "This will simply be a superficial Family Therapy with your mother."

I didn't really know what she meant. Therapy is supposed to be anything but superficial. And the last time I heard from my mom, she was yelling at me.

On the other end, the phone rang and rang but no one picked up. Finally, my mom picked up. "I'm sorry about the phone, I went upstairs for a minute and for some reason I thought that you were going to call tomorrow."

My mom sounded happy. I knew she missed me and I felt bad that I hadn't written her as much as I should have. She really cared about me.

"Judy, I told you it was today and reminded you three times," Miss Fawn said.

"So Abby," my mom ignored Miss Fawns' remark, "did you watch the Huskies play the other day?" I was relieved my mom didn't start an argument with Miss Fawn.

"We don't have television here, Mom."

The superficial conversation lasted not even two minutes when my mom said, "So Abby, I was up in your room the other day and I was thinking about the year you lived with me and the times we had. And I want you to know that when you come home, you have the choice to live with me."

Miss Fawn interrupted, "Judy, I told you specifically that you were not to bring that up."

"I'm her mother and I have the right to talk to my daughter! I see that he's gotten to you, did he pay you off too?"

Miss Fawn snapped, "This conversation has to come to an end. Abby, hang up."

I hung up the phone hearing my mom screaming, "You have no right. I'm her moth —".

I just sat there not knowing how to feel, think, or act. I felt guilty that I didn't stand up for my mom because she needed me. But I also understood what my dad was doing. My soul was being split in two and I just felt numb.

TIME: 10:38 pm   **PATIENT NAME: Abigail Vona**

Milieu treatment note: Patient continues to sit and attempt to suck her thumb and wrap her pointer finger around her nose.

- T. Grout

Day 304

We worked in the garden in the rain for hours. My clothes were drenched. All afternoon Miss Grout held her umbrella over her head and twirled it around singing, "Singing in the rain, just singing in the rain. . ." She didn't know any other lyrics, just repeated it over and over again. If it wasn't for Miss Grout's pleasant voice, silly gestures, and that she is a great person, I would have found her irritating.

"Put away your shovels," said Miss Rossly. "We're going back to the cabin. I have an announcement, and I can't stand this rain." I never was more grateful to get back in the cabin and into some warm clothes. Miss Rossly waited for us to get dressed and sit in a half-circle with Miss Grout.

"Rochelle, you're ready to go home and will be leaving tomorrow."

I felt as if someone had grabbed my heart from my chest. I became very upset. Rochelle took her departure hard too. It was like a death sentence for her. She put her head deep in her lap, her hands ripping at her hair.

"I can't leave! I'm not ready!" she gasped in between her sobs. The Staff knew how hard Rochelle would take this. Rochelle's stay here was similar to a refuge. She was hiding from her past, Joaquin, and her addictions. Her addiction became The Village and she didn't want to leave it.

"You're ready to go," Miss Rossly said, trying to calm Rochelle down.

"You need to face your fears and grow as a person. You're ready. We can't help you anymore."

Rochelle lifted her head, but her face was a blur through my own tears. I felt like she was a mirror and I was looking at myself. She was more than a best friend to me. Rochelle and I had been there with each other through all of our treatment so we had a special bond.

That night I prayed for the first time in my life. I prayed for something that wasn't about me. I prayed for Rochelle. I asked God to keep her away from Joaquin, coke, and any other trouble. I prayed for her to have strength. I didn't feel corny or weak asking God for those things. And after I prayed, surprisingly, I gained courage too. I felt better about letting her go.

The next day during lunch, a tall, dark woman who looked no older than thirty came into the cafeteria. She was rather pretty and looked like an older, darker version of Rochelle: full lips, slanted big eyes, and high cheekbones.

Rochelle looked happy to be going home with her mother, but I felt like she took a part of me with her.

Individual Psychotherapy note: Abigail continues to feel hopeless and despondent about the difficulties she is experiencing in her treatment. She once again made the connection that her "regression" in progress seemed to have occurred while on a visit with her mother. Despite this connection Abigail was very resistant to exploring this further.

- Dr. K. Wisely

Chapter 9

TEMPTATION

Day 307

I sat in the passenger seat while Miss Rossly drove me to the airport. She turned on the radio and found a country station. I was nervous but I felt strong and good. I looked over at Miss Rossly. She was beautiful in this natural way. She seemed not to care about how she looked and I think that made her more pretty. I admired her for that and wanted to be like her.

Miss Rossly left me at the terminal with my boarding pass. "Good luck," she said and then walked away. I could do whatever I wanted. I could use the pay phone, I could run. But in the end, I got on the plane and sat in my seat. I was going home. It was just for a weekend, but my stomach had a funny, nervy feeling that just stayed there.

I sat in my seat next to a middle-aged businesswomen. I didn't talk with her because I was uncertain whether I would be breaking any rules.

Before I was allowed to leave I had to memorize dozens of rules. Rules like: no jewelry, no makeup, no platform shoes, no going off schedule . . . it was endless.

I had to spend the days leading up to my visit making a schedule of what I would be doing every minute of my day there.

This was a precaution that went along with going off-campus. I had to change the schedule at least seven times before Miss Strickler approved it.

My dad met me in the airport at baggage claim. It was funny seeing people walking around with cell phones, chatting, going here and there very fast. It contrasted with my life at The Village. The people sounded harsh to me now; I liked the sing-song of southern accents and how polite everyone was.

My house looked the same. Actually, it smelled a lot better — the odor of pot mixed with B.O. that usually came from the basement was gone now that my brother wasn't here. But all wasn't good when I arrived in my room. I counted at least nine things that were missing, including my TV. I didn't say anything. I knew my brother stole it when he went to college. I just hoped that I would get it back in one piece when I came back home. If I came back home.

The rest of the day was spent doing things that I used to do as a child, like playing miniature golf in the back and watching movies that were PG-13. One of the rules was that I couldn't go anywhere where I might run into my old friends.

This was a rule I didn't mind. If I ran into anyone that I used to hang out with then I would hide. I looked like shit and was ashamed about all the gossip that would be going around about how I had returned from this crazy place down south.

When my dad and I were at the Ground Round eating dinner, I started to have a bad stomach pain. I tried to go on with the night, telling my dad it was a cramp but it didn't go away and during the movie that night I had to run to the bathroom. When it was time for bed I had a fever.

I lay in bed listening to my dad talk to one of my Staff from The Village.

The Village was very strict about what meds to give kids and I knew that's what they were talking about. Some kids take meds to get high. I remember Mary telling us how she tried to get drunk from drinking NyQuil — why anyone would do that I don't know because it tastes like shit.

My dad came in with a glass of water and two pills. The Village probably had to approve them.

I woke up the next day feeling a lot better. I wondered if my sickness was psychosomatic, from coming home. "Dad, where are you?" I yelled but no one was there. I didn't like this and I knew that I was breaking a rule by not doing what I was assigned to do at that time. When I opened the refrigerator I noticed there was a note. "Abby, I'm out running errands. Get some sleep and I'll see you later. I got some bagels and cream cheese for you. Hope you like that. Dad."

I didn't mind that he was out. The thing I had a problem with was that this was breaking a rule. I wasn't supposed to be left alone. It was one of the most important rules. I knew that when I got back, Staff would probably yell at me.

I sat at the kitchen table and ate my bagel. This was the first time in a long time that I had to eat alone.

I thought about my Step Nine, "To make amends whenever possible except when injuring people." I wondered if I should make amends with Matt for cheating on him, or Anastasia for taking a big chunk of her wardrobe then blaming it on a girl I didn't like. When I had brought it up with the Group the day before, Ally said, "Having anything to do with people you partied with is bad, even if you do something good. It will make you relapse."

Then Miss Strickler told me, " One of the rules for the Steps is that you can't have a boyfriend until you wait a year, then you buy a plant. If that lives, you can get a dog, and if that lives, then you can get a boyfriend. It's a way to measure how much control you have over your recovery." I had nodded but I didn't like the rule. You would have to wait at least two years before you date someone. It didn't seem like a rule that anyone would follow, except Miss Strickler.

I went back to my room and tried to nap but I had slept a lot the night before and wasn't tired. I turned on the TV, but nothing was on. After being away from TV for so long I had lost my taste for it. During a commercial, I went through my things. I tried on my old clothes. Nothing fit.

At The Village we weren't allowed to weigh ourselves because of all the anorexics, so I weighed myself for the first time in almost a year — I had gained thirty pounds! I walked over to my full mirror. At The Village there were no mirrors at all — staff didn't want us to focus on the physical part until we fixed the mental part. I stood in front of the mirror naked, examining my bloated body. I had been a lot smaller the last time I looked at myself.

I wanted my old body back.

I moved closer and looked at my face. Even it looked different. My eyebrows were thicker than they used to be. I picked up my tweezers and started to pluck. *Staff won't notice,* I told myself.

But a little tweeze turned into a drastic change. I knew I would have to come up with something to explain why my eyebrows shrunk in size. I stood in front of the mirror trying to come up with good excuses but couldn't think of any. Fuck it, I thought, and started to apply makeup.

Before I knew it I had shaved my legs, put in my belly ring, and put on an outfit that Miss Strickler would have described as "skanky."

I looked all over my room for eyeliner but I couldn't find it. I decided to go to my sister's room and see if she borrowed it during one of her visits home.

My sister's room was the smallest bedroom in the house. It was also used as the guest room and for storage. It was a plain room with a Madonna picture calendar that she had hung up.

As I was going through my sister's drawers I stumbled across letters that were addressed to me. They were all opened and recently sent to The Village. I wondered why my sister had them in her drawer, but she did lots of unexplainable things.

I shuffled through them. Three were from Matt and the other ones were from Kim and Anastasia. I went back to my room and lay on my bed reading the letters from Matt. They were all in floral envelopes that he must have borrowed from someone.

The first was a sappy love letter that went on for two pages. The second was a paranoid letter with questions like, "Why aren't you answering? Are you cheating?" The third was another love letter. I was surprised he sent me the letters, I didn't even know he could write.

I missed Matt. He wasn't like other guys, I told myself, he wasn't so bad. I wanted to see if he had changed. Maybe he would understand and accept who I was now.

It was four P.M. and my dad still hadn't come back. He had no right leaving me for this long. He knew the rules and he was the one who thought that the rules were a good thing. He sent me to The Village in the first place!

I put in *Beetlejuice*. I needed a happy movie. I eyed my phone. I could call anyone. Staff would never know. The only thing holding me back was that I would have to go back to The Village. I didn't have to tell them. *And* I would working be on Step Nine — I could make amends to Matt and to Anastasia.

I reached for the phone and dialed Matt's number.

Group Treatment note: Patient expressed feeling frustrated and called time to discuss her action plans for her upcoming visit home. Patient discussed plans for dealing appropriately with negative friends. She also discussed possible compulsions to use makeup, manipulate, sneak out of the house, and engage in inappropriate behavior.

                                             - Dr. K. Wisely

Chapter 10

BLACK OUT

"Yo," said Matt, picking up the phone.

Yo? I didn't like being greeted with "Yo." I had trouble finding my voice. "Hey, it's me, Abby." A rush of what-ifs ran through my head — what if he forgot me, what if he has a girlfriend, what if he doesn't like me anymore?

"Jesus damn . . ." There was an uncomfortable pause, "Where have you been? When did you get back in town? I thought you were gone for good."

I had trouble deciding what I should answer. This was one of the moments I wished I had telepathy so he could just read my mind so I didn't have to explain ten million things and I could read his mind and see if he rejected me or not.

A part of me wanted to hang up the phone. I was digging my grave and when I got back to The Village, they would kill me and bury me in it.

"I just came back. I'm here just for the weekend then I go back."

"Go back?! I heard from my friend who was chilling with your brother that your parents didn't send you to no summer camp, that they shipped you to a mental hospital where they perform some sort of brain surgery and hypnotism shit."

I hated what people thought about The Village. "It's a 'level-three lockdown' and 'tough love' boot camp, with therapeutic traits and a Twelve-Step theme." But it was much more than that.

The conversation went on, with Matt venting his anger about how I was gone for a year and calling my dad an asshole. Then he talked about the weekend he spent in jail. He wanted to come over right then and show me how he fought off two big black guys all by himself but I told him my dad might come home and explained the rules to him. But he went right on talking about what a crazy, fucked-up place I had gone to.

I dropped the phone a couple of times while I was pacing my room talking to Matt. My arm was shaking and I was starting to feel dizzy. I couldn't believe I was doing this. He made plans to come over late. I wanted to say "no." I pictured him breaking into my house at two in the morning and my dad finding out.

I decided to go along with it. I wanted to see what I had missed. I wanted to give him a chance for closure. Anyway, I had broken half the rules so far, fuck it, why not have a little fun. And this *was* Step work. But then I would have to apologize for cheating on him, and I really didn't know when I was going to find the time to do that.

He told me he was going to come by after midnight.

My dad came home around seven. It was starting to get dark and if I hadn't felt guilty about breaking the rules I would have been mad at him. But in a way we were even — he broke rules and I broke rules. I almost told my dad about Matt when we were playing a board game. I was also worried that if I had this much guilt around my dad then I would have even more around my Group. It would be almost impossible to keep things from them. They knew me so well, and Miss Strickler had a special ability when it came to finding people's dark little secrets.

When it was time for bed I opened my window so I could hear

Matt when he came. Then I turned off my lights and sat in bed waiting. STU had helped instill patience in me.

Around midnight I heard Prince barking then I heard, "Psst, Abby." Matt was standing below my window smoking a cigarette.

"Put out the cigarette before I come down." I didn't want Staff to smell smoke on my clothes. That would be a really stupid thing to get in trouble for.

I tiptoed down the stairs, being more careful than I ever had before. There was more at stake now if I got caught. I mean, at that point, I might as well run away for good because they would probably put me on STU for the rest of my days.

When I got outside, Matt and I approached each other. It had been a long time since I looked at a boy that I would consider fucking.

He looked the same. I used to look at him as an investment — I had thought that he would be really hot when he grew out of his baby face and stretched a couple inches. But the only thing that had grown was his poor attempt at facial hair, which didn't suit him. His baby fat had turned chunky. I was disappointed. I had expected him to change in a good way, not a bad one.

But when we hugged each other and I was wrapped in his arms I didn't care, I missed him.

We decided to walk to Anastasia's house. Her mother was gone and she was throwing a party. This didn't seem like something Anastasia would do, she was always so cautious before.

As we walked, Matt tried to kiss me.

"I want to, but . . ." I couldn't really put into words why I didn't want to kiss him and even if I could he wouldn't understand. If I kissed him, I would have even more trouble leaving him and, when I went back The Village, I'd get in even more shit than I was in right now.

After no more than five minutes of walking, Matt pulled out his cell phone. "I'm callin' a cab. I don't want to walk this much."

This was the first time I saw how truly lazy Matt was — a seven minute walk, and he could use the exercise. I chose to keep my mouth shut.

In the cab, Matt told me how he quit his job working at his family's bakery. "I've been working for Ben the last six months. It pays real well." The only Ben that Matt and I both knew was my ex-boyfriend, the town drug dealer. For a second I thought of asking what business Ben had opened. My isolation from the world had made me naive. Matt was Ben's little sidekick drug dealer now. I didn't want to talk to him anymore. The whole thing made me ill.

Just then we pulled in front of Anastasia's house. There was a group of kids gathered, holding beers on the front lawn, and a girl lying down — probably a wasted freshman. I recognized some of the kids and felt like running away. The last thing I wanted was for them to recognize me and then have it get around town and have my brother find out. My brother would like nothing better than to be the bearer of bad news and tell my dad what I was up to.

Matt swore at the cab driver, saying, "You ripped me off, you fucker!" I tried to think of a way for me to go into Anastasia's house without someone recognizing me. "I want to go home," I whispered to Matt, giving up on the whole thing and wishing I never came, never called him, never plucked my eyebrows.

"Chill," he said.

I didn't, I just pictured him with Ben selling pot to little kids and him looking up to Ben like some kind of mentor. I must have been dreaming to think I liked him. Boy, we would make a good couple: an NA fanatic and a drug dealer.

The front door of the house flung open hitting the side causing a huge bang. A guy carrying a girl stumbled through it, almost falling. The guy was a football player who had graduated from my school two years before and was still at high school parties. It took me longer to recognize the girl — it was Anastasia, only she had cut her hair, caked on makeup, and was wearing a bathing suit with heels. She was laughing and very drunk. The guy put her down and they walked toward us. I was shocked at how much she had changed. She was too drunk to notice me as she tried to get to the guy's car.

I didn't want to talk to her. And I didn't want to continue to talk to Matt.

"Hey Anastasia, look who's here," Matt yelled.

I wanted to run.

"Who's here? Who are you?" Anastasia started to laugh hysterically as the guy tried to pull her into his car. "Get off, Allen! I wanna see who it is." She fell down, then laughed. She walked closer to us. Her skin was orange from self tanner, she had put on a lot of black eyeliner to make her eyes look dramatic, and her bikini with heels made her look like an upper-class porn star. She had a jaded, worn look, no more fresh pretty innocence.

I was four feet from her. She squinted to try to figure out who I was.

"Hi Anastasia."

"Oh my God, look at you!" She checked me out head to toe in a pointless examination that she would not remember in the morning. She told me how much I had changed, swearing that I had picked up a southern accent. I wondered if I had or if she was just drunk and delusional.

I wanted to leave right then but curiosity got the better of me. Now that I had gone this far, I wanted to find out what had happened to the rest of my friends.

"So, how's Kim?" I asked, going right into drunk gossip mode.

"Kim dropped out and got a job with her mom working at Filene's. Her mom got fired, right after Kim was hired, for stealing the clothes. That's why she had damn nice outfits, because they steal them. They had to move out of state and no one's heard from them since."

When I asked about Nate and Adam, there was a silence from every one.

"Nate was driving his car like four months ago and got into an accident. There was a service at school and everything. Adam is inside. He just got out of some sort of rehab for coke or heroin or something. He's a total burnout."

The guy, Allen, came up behind Anastasia. "Let's bounce," he said. This time Anastasia went off with him, stumbling all over her stiletto heels.

The whole thing depressed me. Matt stood there trying to make sexy faces that didn't fit him.

"I have to go," I said.

He looked at me like I was crazy. "Come on, just for a little, check it out. Been a real long time since we hung out." He didn't get it and I didn't want to explain it to him because he still wouldn't get it.

I tried to figure out the best way to leave without him chasing me and without me having to hurt his feelings. "I have to go," I said flatly and turned around and left. Then I ran all the way to my house.

I snuck in, regretting the whole thing, wishing I was at The Village, wanting them to hide me from all this shit. I hit my bed with my fists, angry with myself.

TIME: 9:14 am   **PATIENT NAME:** Abigail Vona

Individual Psychotherapy note: Abigail was seen for one 45-minute session. Abigail discussed several violations of rules while on her home visit. She expressed worry and anxiety about her staff's reaction as she had not yet informed them of the rule violations. She outlined with therapist her plan to inform her father and staff and take responsibility for these actions.

- Dr. K. Wisely

Day 310

Miss Strickler greeted me at The Village entrance. It was just the two of us, walking to the garden site where the rest of the Coyotes were working.

"So, how was your visit home? And how was everything with your dad? You didn't run into any problems?"

My fingernails were turning red and bloody from biting them. "Fine."

Miss Strickler stopped walking, "Your behavior right now is behavior you showed when you first walked though STU's door. You're biting your nails — something happened. Did you see your mother?"

I wished that I could say "yes." Right then, everything that had to do with my mom was so little compared to this. Then I broke. I couldn't keep this secret. Not because it was so big but because it scared me and I didn't want to deal with it.

I told her the whole thing trying to stop my nervous laugh. I was surprised that she didn't say anything. I didn't know if her silence was a good thing or bad. We just kept walking.

When we arrived at the garden site, Katherine and Ally were

especially happy to see me.

"Stop," Miss Strickler said. "Come over here. I have an announcement to make."

Twenty minutes of guilt trips. Twenty minutes of Ally crying. Twenty minutes of Candace scolding me.

I was at the bottom again. Even Candace was better than me. It was especially hard because just that last Friday I had been the most trusted, I had been the most respected, and now Miss Strickler would make comments just like she did when I told about stealing: "Abby, tell the Group, did you have sex?" or "Watch her, Miss Rossly, she might sneak off to see her drug-dealer boyfriend."

I just shoveled the rest of the afternoon.

TIME: 9:57 pm   **PATIENT NAME: Abigail Vona**

Patient required staff assistance to stop picking at herself today. Patient remains in gloves due to persistent scratching and picking at herself. Patient complied with all staff directives and Black Out guidelines throughout the day.

- B. Rossly

Day 311

Staff had "treatment team" in the morning. We weren't supposed to know about it, but we did. It was when Staff got together to decide their agenda and our Consequences, or "special interventions." I feared that they might put me back in STU.

Dr. Wisely met with us for Group. He shook his head and looked at me. Then he started asking me question after question. He turned to the Group.

"Do you notice that she doesn't show feeling?"

The Group nodded their heads.

"You've completely cut yourself off, Abby."

I nodded, feeling more guilty.

"You regressed all the way to the beginning of your treatment, and you regressed a while ago, not just with this."

I didn't nod. I didn't know what he was talking about.

"It started with Family Therapy, with your mother."

I looked at him like he was crazy.

"You can't let go of her, and the guilt you feel consumes you."

I didn't get what he was saying, and if I did, I didn't agree with it.

Dr. Wisely shook his head, "You need time to reflect, Abby. You will be on 'Black Out' until you start seeing things clearly."

There was an "ahhh," from Ally. She knew what Black Out was and I had heard about it. It is the very worst kind of Consequence or treatment team decision. All you do, all day, every day, until they decide to take you off, is nothing. Just think and reflect. Like solitary confinement on the outside.

I could not have any contact with the Group, not even Group Therapy. I couldn't have Family Therapy either, so I couldn't find out how my dad reacted to my behavior. I was only allowed to eat, drink, shower, and follow the Group. This made STU look very easy.

I thought a lot about my mom, all the good memories and the bad. She wasn't terrible like they said, she was just her own person. Dr. Wisely was right though, I didn't want to give her up and it killed me to think of the pain she went through when she couldn't see me. After all, she was my mom, and no one is perfect.

TIME: 4:33 pm   PATIENT NAME: Abigail Vona

Milieu Treatment note: Patient also continues to appear disheveled and unkempt. At meal times patient eats very little — two to three

bites per meal. Patient remains on Black Out due to unsafe behaviors and consistent rule-breaking.

- T. Grout

Day 312

A week went by and the only thing that happened of any significance was when a stray dog came over to me and sat down. Miss Strickler yelled, "You get three hundred push-ups if you even think about petting that dog." She then game me fifty push-ups for looking at the dog.

TIME: 7:14 pm   **PATIENT NAME: Abigail Vona**

Milieu Treatment note: Patient remains on personal Black Out per doctor's orders. She will be assessed by a representative of the treatment team every few days to decide to continue Black Out. At this time, Abby will remain on Black Out due to her continuing negative impact on the group by endangering them, lying, and manipulating the rules.

- N. Strickler

Day 319

Finally, after more than a week, Dr. Wisely allowed me back into Group Therapy. I was off Black Out. Joining the group, I felt like an outcast freak with leprosy. Ally understood because she had gone through the same thing.

"Did you give any thought to what I said about your mother?" Dr. Wisely asked.

I nodded my head, "I have, and I know that you're right. I don't like to think of my mom as crazy. I don't think it's true and I'm angry at you and angry at my dad and Miss Fawn for pointing out how I can't be around her and how she isn't a good example for me."

Dr. Wisely looked pleased, this was the response he was looking for — the truth.

"When I think back to my visit home, I used my dad breaking the rules to sabotage things. Then I justified it with the Steps." Everyone looked confused. "Never mind," I said, realizing that telling them how I was really on a mission for Step Nine was ridiculous. "In a way, I don't regret what I did. I know now that I don't want to go back to the way when I was unhappy and always looking for approval. I think that I want to find a new life and if I smoke, drink, steal, or hang out with my old friends, it won't be fun anymore. It will remind me of my struggles."

"So are you're saying that you don't feel bad for lying to your dad and sneaking out?" asked Candace, trying to corner me.

"No, that's not what I meant. I feel bad for sneaking out. But I feel worse for letting you all down."

A relationship with parents is a strong one but not always a good one. You have such a close bond with them, and when you change, you expect them to change with you, or be able to support and guide you. It is sad when you out-grow your parents like I did my clothing. You feel vulnerable to the world without them there and you don't have the support you need. You can go through your whole life waiting for them to grow up like you have, using their lack of responsibility as an excuse. Or you can get on with your life, like Ally is trying to do, like I am trying to do.

TIME: 5:28 pm   **PATIENT NAME: Abigail Vona**

Group Treatment note: Patient explained that she had been thinking about her negative behaviors while on Black Out and stated, "It is easier to say that I don't care than to worry about what I did. I feel like there's nothing I can do to get my dad to take me home now."

- Dr. K. Wisely

Chapter 11

TOXIC WASH

Day 320

I had a two-hour Family Therapy. During the session, my dad listened to me apologize and cry. At the end of the session Miss Fawn said, "Abby, I don't think that your sneaking out was a bad thing, because you learned from it. Your dad and I have given some thought to a change in plans. We think that perhaps you should attend boarding school on your discharge. It might be a better place for you to live."

I didn't think boarding school was a bad idea. I would get away from the people in my town, my mom, and my brother. Boarding schools did have some drawbacks though. The kids sent were usually flawed in some way — there was a reason their parents didn't want them living at home. Like me.

As time went on, I quickly climbed back into being one of the most trusted peers. I felt better about my visit home. Miss Fawn was right. I had learned from my mistakes and I felt stronger emotionally. It made me think about what Austin had told me, "Wisdom only comes with pain and misfortune."

I was given back the title and responsibilities of Group Leader. Miss Strickler said that I got it because I needed to practice handling life.

I was back to my old self in the Group. Family Therapy was going well, and I found out things about my stepmom that I never knew and even admired. She told me how she practiced yoga, and when she was in college she was a belly dancer. I wanted to learn to do both of these things. She said she couldn't wait until I came home so she could teach me. I pictured her belly dancing. Boy, did she have a belly. I wondered if her double chin shook when she moved. But despite her physical flaws, she was pretty and probably danced beautifully.

Miss Fawn asked me if I had any plans for summer. I had planned to be at The Village. This told me that I might be getting out soon. Now that home seemed so close, I couldn't decide if I truly wanted to go back. I started to fear going back. The Village was now my protection from the world. Everything was pure here. There were no wolves in sheep's clothing. Even when one of us was pretending to be something or someone else, we all knew who they really were. I knew every one of my peers inside out. This was better than the family and friends I had. Out in the real world, there's so much bullshit.

Then sometimes I would think just the opposite. I wanted them to get it over with and boot me out now.

TIME: 7:42 pm   **PATIENT NAME: Abigail Vona**

Patient described a new intention to "support" herself, stating, "I don't know why." Patient related this intention to her relationship with her mother, describing it as "enmeshed" and "not a healthy relationship for me." Patient seemed to pause frequently in order to collect her thoughts or maintain focus.

                                                            - Dr. K. Wisely

Day 322

After almost a month of neglecting my Step work, I finally decided to work Step Eleven: "Seek through prayer and meditation to improve our conscious contact with God as we understand Him, praying for only the knowledge of His will for us and the power to carry that out." This was hard because I wasn't used to praying or meditating and didn't really know how to work this Step.

I wished that I was a more religious person, but the truth is I was a confused person who was not really sure if there was a God. So if I did like some aspects of religion, it was the parts about how to live your life for happiness and for other people in trying to find God.

TIME: 6:31 pm   **PATIENT NAME: Abigail Vona**

Group Treatment note: Patient expressed feeling withdrawn, guilty, hurt, frustrated, miserable, meek, and discouraged. Patient expressed "My past six years have been very lonely. I didn't want to go home feeling lonely. Don't know how to change it. Work and Treatment, I guess. I think I have to find ways to create happiness."

- Dr. K. Wisely

Day 323

"Katherine," Miss Grout said, putting a plump arm on Katherine's shoulder, "I just got some terrible news. Your grandfather died last night. I'm so sorry." Katherine looked completely devastated.

She collapsed into Miss Grout's outstretched arms. The thing I loved about Miss Grout was her never-ending love for us. She wasn't afraid to show us how much she cared. I couldn't see Miss Strickler holding Katherine like that to calm her down. "Oh, Katherine," Miss Grout said as Katherine cried softly in her arms.

I knew Katherine was very close to her grandfather. She talked about how he used to take her out for ice cream. She wanted him to be proud of her. Katherine took the news hard and kept to herself.

That night at the bathhouse, I heard a gag coming from the shower next to me, then a cough following another gag. It didn't sound like throwing up but it did sound suspicious. The bad thing was that Katherine was in the stall next to me. I stepped out of my shower with soap suds all over me and grabbed a towel.

"Miss Rossly," I whispered, panicky. I didn't want any of the Group members to hear.

"What are you doing?"

"I heard strange sounds from the stall next to me. Katherine is in there."

"What kind of sounds?" Now she was panicked too, with the same premonition I had.

"Like coughing, only gurgling, like she swallowed something harsh."

"Showers off now! And all of you step out so I can see you," Miss Rossly ordered, taking the situation even more seriously than I predicted.

Every girl, even Candace, quickly stepped out, except Katherine, who dropped a bottle of something that rolled and then hit a wall.

When Katherine finally came out, Miss Rossly quickly headed over to her shower stall. Katherine looked ill. The color in her skin had drained out. Her lips were pressed together like she was holding something in her mouth. I couldn't tell if it was a grief-stricken look or something worse. Miss Rossly picked up what looked to be a bottle of anti-pimple wash that was empty.

"This was full when I got it out for you today," Miss Rossly said, examining Katherine suspiciously. Katherine's pale face was sweating. "I dropped it and it spilled down the drain."

We all knew she was lying. We all knew she must have drunk it. Could face wash kill you if you consumed an entire bottle?

Miss Rossly read the warning label on the bottle carefully. Then she grabbed the phone and dialed. I didn't hear the conversation. Miss Grout had us stay in the shower because of all the men coming into the bathhouse. Being used to a five-minute shower, a forty-five minute shower seemed so luxurious. When my feet and fingers became wrinkly, Miss Grout ordered, "Showers off!"

When the Group was back at the cabin, Miss Grout called us over.

"Katherine swallowed a fair amount of toxic face wash." The Group couldn't believe it, except me. I already knew.

"Is she going . . . to . . . die?" Ally asked.

"No, no, not that serious. It wasn't enough and it's not powerful enough to take someone's life."

Katherine was always so glum. Once Miss Grout told her to throw rocks at Rochelle's porta at night as a joke — when Rochelle came out all panicked, Katherine actually laughed with everyone, but that was the only time. She was incapable of relating to us when we were telling jokes or having fun. She only talked and related to us when we were in the depths of depressing issues. I hoped she got through this.

TIME: 10:52 pm   **PATIENT NAME: Abigail Vona**

Milieu Treatment note: In the evening patient stated, "I feel like I'm crazy and I'm going to be like this forever."

                                        - N. Strickler

Day 324

    If suicide attempts weren't such a serious matter, I would have found Katherine's incident funny. Funny that she swallowed face wash; and funny that it wasn't even poisonous enough to kill you. But the reasons behind it, the pain she must have felt over her grandfather's death, these weren't amusing in the slightest. We all felt gloomy about Rochelle's departure and Katherine's suicide attempt.

    One night I was reading my meditation for the day when a thought occurred to me. What if I asked permission to read it in the morning to the Group? The quotes were meditations to enjoy and live life by. They were corny but they were good. And it would also count as my Step Eleven.

    When I asked Miss Strickler about it, surprisingly she said, "Yes, but you have to get up three minutes earlier."

    At first the Group, especially Candace, didn't approve of getting up three minutes earlier, but the meditation seemed to lift our spirits and make me feel better, not only about myself, but about life. Little things help. I felt like the cabin minister. Maybe I did believe in God.

TIME: 7:57 pm   **PATIENT NAME: Abigail Vona**

Group Treatment note: Patient called time to talk about her parents and stated "I don't feel as close to my mother as I used to. I don't feel as close to my father which is strange. Now everything is changing. I have a lot to think about."

                                           - Dr. K. Wisely

Chapter 12

CANDY

Day 325

M iss Fawn told me, "Now that we knocked down the old house of your relationships together, and made a new foundation, we can start planning to build your house into a home." I thought this analogy was a little out there, and Miss Fawn sounded more like an interior decorator than a therapist. But once I got over the home part, literally, I knew exactly what she was talking about.

My dad, my stepmom, and I got along all right therapeutically, but we needed to come up with plans for when I got home. My stepmom took this very seriously, trying to come up with a plan for my future. I was going to be going to a small boarding school in Massachusetts. And if I got out before then, Dad would find me a job in his office.

We were discussing family vacations in Bermuda and getting another dog when Miss Fawn cut my father off.

"Abby, how are you going to deal with your old friends and boyfriend, Matt?"

This was something I didn't really want to face. It was a subject that was brought up over and over again after my visit home. I made a decision to drop Matt and go solo for a year, like all the AA and NA books recommended.

I didn't really care for some of my friends when it came down to it. Others I wanted to see when I came home. My dad wanted to put a restraining order on Ben, my ex-boyfriend. I didn't see the point of this because we had broken up over a year before, but my dad said Ben had called the house looking for me. Ben was one person I didn't want to deal with. After we had broken up, I heard rumors of him getting arrested for shipping ecstasy from New York and for carrying guns. I knew about his gun collection, which made him especially scary. He was crazy enough to carry a loaded gun and use it.

I thought about my friends and how they could get me back in trouble and I decided I had to start from scratch. The past seemed like an unfinished dream, not unfinished reality.

TIME: 7:37 pm   **PATIENT NAME: Abigail Vona**

Group Treatment note: Patient checked into the Group Treatment as feeling "sad and depressed." Patient stated, "One of my fears of going home is my brother. I admired him a lot and I tried to impress him by smoking weed and stealing. It is going to be tempting because his friends are going to be there. I'm afraid I am going to lose who I am here. It's going to be hard." Patient appeared content and seemed clear. Patient gave positive feedback to her peers.

- Dr. K. Wisely

Day 326

I read Step Twelve, my last step: "Continue to follow these Steps whenever possible." It's not really a Step, more of a reminder.

In a way, at that moment, I knew I was finished here.

I had noticed for a while that I hadn't been growing anymore.

I had reached my potential. This place wasn't a challenge now. You know when you learn as much as you can from a place, because you don't feel uncomfortable any longer. When something is new and challenging, you may not feel up for it, but when you're finished and look back, you're glad you did it, however much you didn't want to. It's just like stretching or working out a muscle. You achieve a certain point in physical health when you need to set your goals higher. My goals now were past the realm of The Village.

The cabin door opened and Miss Strickler stepped in. Behind her was a pale, beautiful girl, no older than fifteen, with blue-green eyes and long lashes. She walked in the room with an inner confidence and superiority. Her left eyebrow lifted when she saw the cabin.

"This is where we live?" she asked, in an English accent, looking at our cabin like it was the most pathetic thing she had ever seen. "No air conditioner?" she asked, batting her luminous eyes at Miss Strickler.

"Listen, Charlotte, you're here for a reason and probably a pretty good one if your mom shipped you off from England. You better improve your attitude or you'll be here for a very, very long time."

Miss Strickler knew how to deal with little bullshitters like Charlotte, like any of us when we first arrived. I no longer looked at Miss Strickler the way I used to, the way Charlotte must have been looking at her now. I was surprised when Miss Strickler asked Charlotte to go on three-foot with Candace.

"Candace will teach you more than the rest of the peers here."

Candace looked confused. So did the rest of the Group. Candace didn't keep track of the rules and would be a terrible three-foot buddy. But then I realized what Miss Strickler was doing.

Candace was the most self-centered girl I knew. And Charlotte from her entrance was Candace's match. They were meant for each other and could probably both learn from the other's faults, if Charlotte didn't get strangled first.

I got to know Charlotte's personality over the next two weeks. What I saw in her were some of the things I recognized in myself. She was self-centered and strong-willed but not outrageous in her attempts to disregard authority. She had no apparent problems beside the fact that she was depressed and extremely selfish. As she talked in Group Therapy about how her mom overate and her dad was a perfectionist, she moved her cat-like eyes in arrogance. She did not get it yet and it would take a while.

I, on the other hand, am becoming a more honest person, unable to lie anymore. I wonder if that makes me more evolved or less evolved.

Why is there so much shit we have to weed out before getting into the things that make up life? In a lifetime, the people you show yourself to are limited. When I was out in the real world, I wore different masks over my personality; masks that were images of what people wanted to see in me, or how I wanted them to view me. I always carried my masks around and hardly ever took them off. I cared so much about what people thought that I lost my identity, if I ever had one in the first place. My masks and my facades were burdens that weighed me down. Over my stay here, I let them go and now my soul feels lighter — still heavy with guilt and regret, but without the constant fear of how people view who I am.

It was hard for me to explain to people then, and still is today, what you go through at The Village. Mentally, you grow very fast, and it's very effective. But also, it was like the movie *Groundhog Day*. You just did the same thing over and over until you got it right, until you *changed*, and then maybe they let you go.

Charlotte was far from getting it right. I would never see her as she really was, and I would not be here long enough to see the person she might become.

TIME: 9:43 am   **PATIENT NAME: Abigail Vona**

Individual Psychotherapy note: During the session Abigail continued to describe her frustration with her current group status. She focused particularly on interactions with her staff, and she described feeling upset as she perceives them as being angry or treating her unkindly. Abigail was genuinely engaged with the therapist; she appeared in a relatively good mood and alert.

- Dr. K. Wisely

Day 327

Miss Strickler circled us up. "Abby . . ."

Did I violate another rule? Or maybe this was more about care-taking.

"We feel that you've learned all you need here. You'll be leaving tomorrow."

The situation I would have killed for a year ago was finally coming true. I stood there, statuesque, frozen in thought, but not able to think clearly. I heard weeping.

"How do you feel?" Miss Rossly asked.

It seemed unreal. I turned to the right of me and saw Ally crying. Katherine was teary-eyed too. I slowly turned my head to the left and saw Candace looking furious that I was getting out, but she was probably glad to be rid of me. And Charlotte was just bored.

I answered, "Ever feel like you're in a dream when you're awake but you know you're awake? It's like, you know, but you don't believe?"

My Group looked back at me blank except for Charlotte, who to my surprise nodded her head.

"I know what you're talking about," she said eagerly. "I get like that when something weird happens."

I felt thankful that someone knew what I was talking about, even if it was Charlotte.

The rest of the day went by and it slowly sank in that I was leaving. I didn't want to. I felt vulnerable. *It's safe here. It's the only place I know where I can be myself and where I actually know who I am.*

TIME: 10:43 am   **PATIENT NAME: Abigail Vona**

Individual Psychotherapist note: Abigail experienced difficulty saying goodbye. Therapist wished Abigail best wishes and said goodbye.

- Dr. K. Wisely

Day 328

"Say goodbye to the Group," said Miss Strickler, like I would see them again that afternoon. Ally and Katherine hugged me.

"Bye," I said to the girls, tears running down my cheeks. "You helped me and I'll think of you." Then I closed the cabin door behind me.

Miss Strickler walked with me. I was glad she had volunteered to take me to the airport. I would miss her. *I will miss all my Staff, and their southern accents too.* I was disappointed that I wasn't able to say goodbye to Miss Grout and Miss Rossly.

At the terminal, Miss Strickler and I sat waiting for the flight attendant to call my seat number. Suddenly, Miss Strickler said, "Wait here a minute," leaving me there teary-eyed and alone.

She came back a few moments later with a bag of candy bars. "Want one?" She reached in the bag.

To me, this was a miracle. Miss Strickler offering me a present of her prized food?

She pulled out a Snickers bar and handed it to me. "You

deserve it," she said, a smile on her face. "You're not a patient anymore so I'm not breaking any rules."

I stopped crying and unwrapped the Snickers. I was proud and content in that moment.

"I know you'll make it," she said, as my seat number was called. "Now go."

"Can I have another . . . for the road?"

Miss Strickler gave me the whole bag. I walked through the gates eating my candy bars. Oh, how I missed candy. *I'm going to eat every kind to see if my taste buds have changed.*

I had changed a lot since my last plane ride a month ago, let alone over the past year. I knew I had to let go of my past and start over. I was going home as a new person and was never going to look back.

I took my seat and relaxed myself by taking a deep breath. With my new eyes, I wanted to see the world.

PENINSULA VILLAGE   Louisville, Tennessee 37777

PROGRESS NOTES   **HOSPITAL NO. 16135**

TIME: 3:45 pm   **PATIENT NAME: Abigail Vona**

Milieu Treatment note: Patient expressed feeling nervous, anxious, and scattered. She called time to discuss going home. Patient stated, "I don't really have feelings, I'm just doing what I need to do, and I'm really hyper and nervous. Usually, I will feel things later, and it will hit me really hard." Patient made plans to talk with her father, make daily structures, find a job, see a psychiatrist, and "study the Koran." Patient appeared to have trouble organizing her thoughts during this session. She did not appear receptive to staff or peer input, and frequently seemed to make unrealistic plans for herself Abigail seemed to shut down and made no further disclosures at this time.

- N. Strickler

AUTHOR'S NOTE

I changed many of the names in this book to protect the privacy of individuals.

I recently visited Peninsula Village. They told me that Rochelle and Ally had come back to visit too. The Village discourages alums from staying in touch after leaving the program so I don't know how the other girls are doing.

Miss Strickler still works at The Village. The rest of the Staff that I knew have left.

The "Progress Notes" throughout the book are culled from over five hundred pages of notes taken by Peninsula Village psychiatrists, psychotherapists, and Staff.

People ask how I was able to write a book since I am dyslexic with severe problems reading and writing (encoding and decoding issues). Fortunately, I have good comprehension skills. No one thought I would ever be capable of writing a book. I wanted to show them.

I started this book two years ago at the special school I attended after I left Peninsula Village. It began as a diary for my creative writing class. As the story developed, people close to me (especially my mom) took an interest and I brought it to the next level. With my mom's help and "spell check," I came up with a rough manuscript.

My agent gave my rough manuscript to Jay McInerney, who was so helpful in referring me to my publisher. After that, I had a six-month crash course in writing and editing, resulting in what you are reading now.

READING GROUP GUIDE

Bad Girl
Confessions of a Teenage Delinquent
Abigail Vona

RuggedLand

"A compelling memoir that's remarkable on several levels . . . a raw, revealing look at the world of rehab. . . . Vona's appeal is based on her bravery, as well as on the vulnerability that led her down such a dangerous road in the first place."—*People*

"You can't help caring for Abigail Vona, the author of this raw memoir about her year-long stay at a wilderness boot camp. A must read for all ex (and current) bad girls."—*Marie Claire*

"This is not just a *Girl, Interrupted*, this is a girl, wild, trapped, defiant, broken, reformed, and ultimately redeemed."—Jay McInerney

About the Book

She thought her dad was taking her to summer camp. But when Abby Vona and her father reached Louisville, Tennessee, she realized he was committing her to boot camp instead—level-three lockdown in fact, in a tough residential treatment facility called Peninsula Village. *Bad Girl: Confessions of a Teenage Delinquent Part* is the true story of the 328 days Abby spent as a patient there, an experience that forced her to painfully exorcise her darkest fears while confronting the truth about her family, her addictions, and herself. This affluent fifteen-year-old had become an outlaw; it would take another band of teenage outlaws, in treatment alongside her, to restore her shattered identity.

Part *Girl, Interrupted*, part *A Million Little Pieces*, this is the searing account of a life lived so far out of control (booze, boys, drugs, stealing, and runaway charges) yet so in sync with the norms of her peers in her East Coast hometown. Giving us a candid tour inside her world, including excerpts from her psychiatric files, Abby reveals the secrets of the Bad Girl sisterhood, from her partners in crime in Connecticut to the hard-core cases she met at Peninsula Village. As part of her recovery process, her every waking and sleeping moments are scrutinized, "behavior modification" is meted out swiftly, and the topics in group therapy can cover everything from one patient's life as a prostitute to concerns with anorexia, violent rage, and self-mutilation.

A book that raises as many questions as it answers, *Bad Girl* is a provocative choice for reading groups. Whether you read Abby's memoir as a portrait of teenage rebellion or a mesmerizing work of recovery literature, this is a journey through extreme terrain. We hope the topics that follow will enhance the ride. For more information about other Rugged Land selections for reading groups, visit us at www.ruggedland.com.

Topics for Discussion

1. In the book's first scenes, does Abby consider herself to be a bad girl? What does it take to impress her circle of friends? Was she a typical twenty-first-century adolescent?

2. What is the effect of the chapter numbers, which reflect a twelve-step countdown? When causes Abby to hit rock bottom? How does her self-image at −12 compare to +12?

3. Abby's point of view rarely matches the POV expressed by her therapists in their progress reports. Her family members also express opposing viewpoints. How can you decipher the truth about Abby? How was she able to decipher it? Is all reality subjective?

4. Peninsula Village patients come from all walks of life. Do poverty and wealth play opposing roles in addiction? Did Abby's affluence contribute to her destructive behavior, or was money even a factor?

5. What did it take for Abby to begin viewing rules as comforting signs that someone cared about her? Did you consider the Village process to be abusive, or could it translate into guidelines for creating a stable home? What's the difference between an orderly environment and an oppressive one?

6. How do Abby's parents (including her stepmother) compare to the Peninsula staff in terms of having her best interests in mind and being good role models? What accounts for the fact that her brother is not required to seek treatment, and that he rejects Abby's transformation?

7. What communication styles are presented in *Bad Girl*, from Keno (whom Abby has difficulty understanding) to the group-therapy leaders? How would you characterize the way Abby communicates with us as she narrates her story?

8. In the notes documenting Abby's progress, the word "dingy" is almost used as a clinical term after Abby describes herself this way when she feels scattered and unable to focus. To what extent is a "dingy" persona useful for a teenage girl? How much of Abby's low self-confidence do you attribute to her learning disabilities, her parents' divorce when she was six, or peer pressure? What is the effect of her role as "dictionary expert"?

9. Why is physical work in a rustic setting a necessary part of the Village program? Is there a healing power in low-tech living?

10. Discuss the *Bad Girl* case studies that are most memorable for you. Do you consider the dangerous habits of these patients to be the result of nature or nurture? Why is Abby particularly drawn to Ally, who cannot resist returning to her cocaine-addicted mother?

11. How would you have responded to Abby's runaway, boozing, boy-chasing behavior if you had been her parent? How would your parents have responded to Abby?

12. During her trial visit home, Abby's father leaves her alone. The lack of boundaries is frightening for her, and she faces severe consequences upon her return to the Village. Was it right for her to face those consequences, or should her father have been the one receiving the reprimand?

13. How would you have fared in a program like the one at the Village? Could the twelve-step process help you with a particular burden? Were you surprised when Abby chose to focus on stealing as her primary addiction?

14. What might have been the reason for Abby's abrupt notice that she was ready to leave? Why was it important that she not have a lengthy period of anticipation? What outcomes would you have predicted for her if she hadn't spent those months at the Village?

15. How bad have you been in your lifetime? What affects your decisions to conform or rebel? How does America define a bad girl? Are the same standards applied to bad boys?

About the Author

Born in West Hartford, Connecticut, Abigail Vona recently graduated the Foreman School in Litchfield, Connecticut, a boarding school serving students with learning disabilities such as ADD and dyslexia. She has also taken classes at the School of Visual Arts in New York City, where she now lives.